Multicultural Literature Collection

LATINO CARIBBEAN LITERATURE

GLOBE FEARON
EDUCATIONAL PUBLISHER

Paramount Publishing

Executive Editor: Virginia Seeley

Senior Editor: Barbara Levadi

Project Editor: Karen Hill

Contributing Editor: Angela Aguirre, Ph.D.
William Paterson College
Wayne, New Jersey

Editorial Developer: Brown Publishing Network, Inc.

Production Editor: June E. Bodansky

Art Director: Nancy Sharkey

Production Manager: Penny Gibson

Production Coordinator: Walter Niedner

Desktop Specialist: José A. López

Marketing Managers: Sandra Hutchison and Elmer Ildefonso

Cover Design: Richard Puder Design

Photo Research: Omni Photo Communications, Inc.

Cover: New York City–Bird's Eye View, by Joaquín Torres-Garcia

Literature and art acknowledgments can be found on pages 152–154.

Printed in the United States of America.
  4 5 6 7 8 9 10   99 00 01

ISBN: 0-835-90612-4

GLOBE FEARON
EDUCATIONAL PUBLISHER
PARAMUS, NEW JERSEY

Paramount Publishing

CONTENTS

Latino Caribbean Population by State, 1990

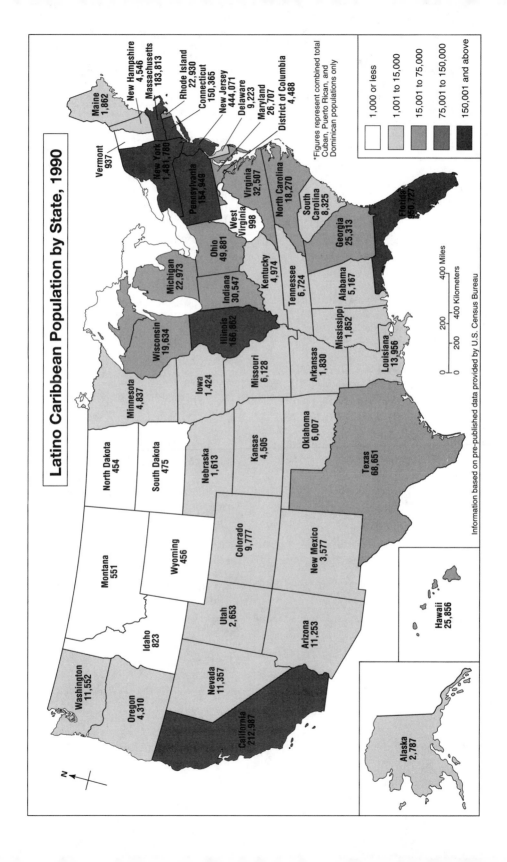

Maine 1,862
New Hampshire 4,546
Massachusetts 183,813
Rhode Island 22,930
Connecticut 150,365
New Jersey 444,071
Delaware 9,223
Maryland 26,707
District of Columbia 4,488
Vermont 937
New York 1,481,780
Pennsylvania 154,946
West Virginia 998
Virginia 32,507
North Carolina 18,270
South Carolina 8,325
Florida 950,727
Ohio 49,881
Kentucky 4,974
Tennessee 6,724
Georgia 25,313
Alabama 5,167
Michigan 22,973
Indiana 30,547
Mississippi 1,852
Illinois 166,862
Wisconsin 19,634
Missouri 6,128
Arkansas 1,830
Louisiana 13,956
Minnesota 4,837
Iowa 1,424
Kansas 4,505
Oklahoma 6,007
Texas 68,651
North Dakota 454
South Dakota 475
Nebraska 1,613
Colorado 9,777
Wyoming 456
New Mexico 3,577
Montana 551
Utah 2,653
Arizona 11,253
Idaho 823
Nevada 11,357
Washington 11,552
Oregon 4,310
California 212,987
Hawaii 25,856
Alaska 2,787

*Figures represent combined total Cuban, Puerto Rican, and Dominican populations only

1,000 or less
1,001 to 15,000
15,001 to 75,000
75,001 to 150,000
150,001 and above

400 Miles
400 Kilometers
200
200
0
0

Information based on pre-published data provided by U.S. Census Bureau.

N

Titles of literature are placed in the time box to reflect, when possible, the historical time or event about which the selections are written.

La Luisa ▼

1868–1878 The Ten Years' War for Cuban independence from Spain is fought, ending in a stalemate.

1886 Slavery is abolished in Cuba.

1899 Following the Cuban-Spanish-American War (1898), Cuba gains independence and Spain surrenders Puerto Rico to the United States.

Little Things Are Big ▼

1917 Jones Act makes all Puerto Ricans citizens of the United States, resulting in a great increase in migration to the U.S. mainland.

1924 U.S. Marines, sent to the Dominican Republic to keep peace, are withdrawn.

1930 Rafael Trujillo gains control of the government of the Dominican Republic.

1933 An army revolt led by General Fulgencio Batista makes him the leader of Cuba.

Raining Backwards ▼

Poem ▼

And Then Came . . . Freedom to Dream ▼

Dedication ▼

Seeing Snow ▼

1950s–1970s Immigration from Puerto Rico to the U.S. mainland reaches a peak.

An Awakening . . . Summer 1956 ▼

1958 The communist revolutionary Fidel Castro overthrows longtime Cuban dictator Fulgencio Batista.

1959 Relations between the Castro government and the United States, which at first were friendly, become strained. Castro looks to the Soviet Union for support in building Cuba's businesses and its military.

1960 About 700,000 middle-class Cubans emigrate, mostly to the United States.

El Doctor ▼

American History ▼

Migrating Notes ▼

1961 President Rafael Trujillo of the Dominican Republic is assassinated.

1963 U.S. President John F. Kennedy is assassinated.

1965 U.S. Marines are sent in to end a revolt in the Dominican Republic.

Latin Jazz ▼

Child of the Americas ▼

In My Country ▼

You Call Me by Old Names ▼

1975 Cuban troops are sent to Angola, a country on the southwest coast of Africa, to help fight South African-backed rebels.

The Diary of a Cuban Boy ▼

1980 Premier Fidel Castro lifts travel restrictions, resulting in the flight of more than 100,000 refugees from Cuba to the United States.

Affirmations #3, Take Off Your Mask ▼

The Great American Justice Game ▼

1980s The U.S. English Organization, led by California Senator Hayakawa, makes efforts to establish English as the official language of the United States.

DEAR STUDENT:

All the cultures that make up the United States have played a major role in shaping the history of this country. In the pages that follow, you will read literature written by people of three Latino Caribbean cultures: Puerto Rican, Cuban, and Dominican. As you read the essays, stories, poems, novel excerpts, diary entry, and play, think about the special traditions, beliefs, and heritages that are part of the Latino Caribbean experience.

The literature in this book is organized into four units. Each unit represents a specific form of literature. The selections in the first unit are factual in nature and focus on personal experiences. The second unit consists of fictional stories based on the rich cultural roots of the authors. The third unit presents two groups of poems. In the first group, the poets reflect on their own identities. In the second group, the poets express their feelings about living in two cultures. The fourth unit presents a play set in a time when it is illegal in the United States to speak any language but English.

The page following the table of contents features a map that shows the Latino Caribbean population throughout the United States. The time box on the facing page provides information about historical events that occurred during the period in which each selection is set.

As you read, think about the writing. The selections represent the experiences of many people who came to this country in the hope of finding a better life. The literature of Latino Caribbeans not only reveals what makes their cultures unique, it also highlights the commonality of all cultures.

UNIT 1

NONFICTION OF THE LATINO CARIBBEANS

Unlike fiction, which involves imaginary characters and events, nonfiction focuses on real life. The characters are real people, the settings are real places, and the events actually happened.

Nonfiction takes many forms, including factual newspaper articles as well as the very personal stories that unfold in biographies and autobiographies. Other forms of nonfiction include letters, diaries, journals, speeches, interviews, newspaper editorials, and essays. An important characteristic of all nonfiction is the inclusion of facts, or information that can be proved to be true. By combining facts with their personal thoughts, feelings, opinions, and values, writers of nonfiction give us insights into the world as they have experienced it.

The first selection in this unit, "The Diary of a Cuban Boy," is taken from a 12-year-old boy's account of his family's experience emigrating from Cuba to the United States. Next is an autobiographical essay titled "Little Things Are Big," in which the writer tells about an experience that shows how prejudice can affect people's natural behavior. In the third selection, "El Doctor," Julia Alvarez relates stories about life with her father, a physician who has achieved success in the United States. Finally, in the excerpt from his autobiography, *Exiled Memories: A Cuban Childhood*, Pablo Medina tells about the times he spent on a Cuban sugar plantation owned by his grandfather. As you read these selections, think about how the authors reveal their thoughts, feelings, and opinions through descriptions of real events and situations.

Puerto Rican artist Victor Lanares captured the feeling of his homeland in his oil painting entitled *Water Bearer*. The artist used bold brush strokes and wide blocks of color with little detail. The viewer sees only a suggestion of the weight of the water pails and the serious mood of the young Puerto Rican boy who carries them. Lanares now lives in New York City and often exhibits his work at El Museo del Barrio there.

INTRODUCTION
The Diary of a Cuban Boy

The following entry is from the diary of a 12-year-old Cuban boy just prior to and shortly after his arrival in the United States in May 1980. In that year, Fidel Castro, the premier—or ruler—of Cuba, lifted emigration restrictions. These restrictions had been put in place because of strained relations between Cuba and the United States. Once restrictions were lifted, more than 100,000 Cubans sailed from Mariel, Cuba, to southern Florida in search of a better life in the United States. Many boats were overcrowded and unseaworthy, which resulted in much suffering and loss of lives. Following their arrival in this country, the immigrants were held in prisons and military camps for months and, in some cases, years.

The diary entry that follows captures the author's feelings about the events surrounding his family's emigration. It reveals his confusion, suffering, shock, unhappiness, and most important, his hope for the future.

The Diary of a Cuban Boy

Anonymous

"I have decided to tell you about a few days in my life. But before I do, I want you to know that my family is a decent and honorable one. We have always been respectable people in our community. Longer than I remember most of us have lived along one street in a small village in Santa Clara province, Cuba. We are a large family with many aunts and uncles and even more cousins. One of my uncles is especially well known because he built many of the houses in our neighborhood. He gave my mother the land for our house. Although this happened many years ago, it is still a topic of conversation in our family.

"This year I started sixth grade in Viet Nam, the Heroic school.[1] I was chosen student leader of the school. I have always been considered a responsible person because I prepare my assignments. My teachers respected me as a good student, not only because I get along well with all the other students but because each day I make sure that the other students prepare their lessons, clean their desks, and have their uniforms and notebooks in order. I follow

---

1. **Viet Nam, the Heroic school** (hih-ROH-ihk SKOOL) probably the name of a specific grade school in Cuba

through with all the activities for the day. During pioneer meetings[2] I have been noticed because I answer all the questions. This past summer I was given a trip to the pioneer camp in Cien Fuegos[3] province where I received a special pioneer course to refresh my mind and to help me perfect my work. At all times I have tried to do my best, both for my teachers and for my parents.

"One day I noticed some strange things happening at home. My mother and father were speaking together in soft voices, quite different from their usual way of speaking. A few days later the pastor of the Baptist church and a friend of our family came for a visit. Although I have always been obedient, when my father sent me to bed, I did not go. I remained silent in the hallway near where everyone was speaking. As I listened, I heard things that I did not like. The pastor said that he had brought along the papers to help my father leave the country. A few days later I overheard another conversation which really startled me. I heard my grandparents discussing the fact that my father had been in jail. I remember those conversations as if they were engraved in my mind. I could not believe it was possible for my father to be considered a criminal. When I asked my grandparents about what I had heard, they would not answer me.

"Later when I asked my mother about what I had heard, she told me everything. She said that my father was a political prisoner on the Isle of Pines. Although he was sentenced to prison for 20 years, when he had served 8 years he was released for good behavior. My mother also explained that since my father had spent the time in

---

2. **pioneer meetings** (py-uh-NIR MEET-ihngz) youth groups organized to foster academic excellence. To become pioneers, students must meet certain academic requirements.
3. **Cien Fuegos** (see-EN FWEH-gohs) a province in Southwestern Cuba

prison before my brother and I were born, she had not told us or anyone else about it because she wanted to spare us problems which she knew that we would encounter if we knew that our father was against the government. The rest of the 20 year sentence, she explained, Father had to repay by working on weekends for the government. I had always believed that Father was doing voluntary work for the government when he left home on the weekends. I had noticed that he did not usually participate in the government marches and rallies, but I thought he was probably just tired from the voluntary work he did. In fact, I had always thought of my father as being a patriotic idealist for giving so much time to the government. Mother reassured me that it was important to set a good example in the school and community. Then she reminded me of the difficulties which we sometimes had in getting food. She said part of that problem was the result of political problems brought on by our father's record.

"Many other strange things happened at our house during this same period. Every night Mother wrote letters asking for help from Cubans we knew in the United States. She was searching for a way for us to get out of the country. One day Father went to the Ministry of the Interior to obtain the necessary papers. In order to do this he needed birth certificates, their marriage certificate, and a copy of his sentence for treason against the government. When I looked at all these papers, I realized that my father had actually been the treasurer of the counter-revolutionary[4] movement.

"The process of obtaining all these papers took about

---

4. **counter-revolutionary** (KOWN-ter-rehv-uh-LOO-shuh-nehr-ee) *adj.* directed toward overthrowing a government or social system established by a revolution

6 months. Finally Father was told to make an appointment to get our passports. He had to stand in line each day for about 3 weeks before he was able to actually have the passport appointment. We waited another 3 months before we were able to get our passports.

"About the time that we received the passports, I was told that I could no longer be the student leader of the school. This news came as a terrible shock. The director said that someone else had to be substituted in my place because my family was going to abandon the country. I loved my school and was dedicated to being a good leader. How was it possible that I was being replaced when I enjoyed helping the teachers and students so much. What a terrible time.

"To make matters worse, someone from our neighborhood came and took inventory of the things we had in our house. We were told we could take nothing out of the country, nor could we sell or give away anything. An exact account of everything in the house had to be made again just before we left so the government could account for all of our possessions.

"The following Saturday as I was walking along our street eating a mango with my friends, my little brother came running up. He told us that the papers had arrived and we had to get ready to leave. Immediately I left with my close friends to say good-bye to my teachers and all the other people in my town who had been dear to me.

"At 5:00 the next morning our family, my grandparents, my parents, my little brother and I took a bus to Havana.[5] We spent the day in front of the immigration center. Since we had no place to stay, we slept in front of the building on an old mattress Mother found.

---

5. **Havana** (huh-VAN-uh) the capital city of Cuba

About midnight we were called to the main office of the immigration building and given exit papers. Then we were taken to the Circle of Patriotic Socialists where we spent the rest of the night sleeping on the ground along with a lot of other people who were waiting to leave. The next day my mother was able to get four small mattresses so we could sleep a little more comfortably. I don't know how my grandparents managed. I believe they suffered a great deal during this period of time. We had no roof to protect us from the rain or the heat of the sun. We had only the clothes we wore, no medicines or any other supplies.

"We remained at the Circle of Patriotic Socialists for four days. Food was expensive and we had only a little money, so we divided the food between the six of us. The only food we could buy was thin cheese sandwiches, soda crackers, caramels, small packets of milk and a few other drinks.

"On the fourth day we were taken to Mosquito, a small port near the Mariel Harbor. The Cuban government officials there told us that when we got to the United States we should tell everyone we were with the group of people who entered the Peruvian Embassy. The Cuban workers emphasized that if we did not say we were with the embassy people, we would have a hard time getting into the United States. I didn't really understand what the officials meant by this until I spoke with other people who were waiting along with us. They explained that many people had tried to leave Cuba by getting into the Peruvian Embassy yard and as a result the United States was letting some Cubans come there to live. As we went through Cuban Customs we were searched. We had to give up the remaining small amount of money we had left. We also had to give them our little bit of gold jewelry.

"In Mosquito we were taken to a military barracks. The accommodations were divided by groups. The Jehovah's

Witnesses and other religious groups were in one area, the common prisoners in another, and the political prisoners in a separate space. Each area was congested with people all crowded together. We stayed in these barracks six more days before we were loaded onto buses and taken to Mariel Harbor where we were led aboard a boat for the United States.

"We were happy when we saw the yacht we were to travel in. My father guessed that it probably held 25 people safely. Unfortunately for everyone, 48 people were crowded into it. Women and small children were located in the middle. Since my brother and I were the oldest of the children aboard, we were permitted to sit with my grandfather and father near the outer edge of the boat. Sometimes it seemed as if the edge of the boat were going below water level because so many people were crowded onto the boat.

"As we left Mariel Harbor, Cuban government boats accompanied us. They stayed with us until we entered international waters. I'm not sure if the following two events were related, but it seemed to me that they might have been. Shortly after the Cuban boats left us, many people became seasick. When I recovered from the first touch of nausea, I realized that my grandfather was very ill. We could not feel his pulse. As we were attending Grandfather, I saw my brother become rigid and then begin to vomit. Fortunately one of the women on the boat happened to be a nurse. She and another woman who helped her, had their hands full trying to take care of everyone. The seasickness caused such a commotion on board the boat that it nearly turned over. The men worked hard to stabilize the boat. Father reminded us that there were no life jackets on the boat. They had been taken off by the Cuban government workers before we left Mariel. To add to our problems, the engine sputtered and ran out of gas. Shortly after the engine stopped, one of the children who had been ill when we started the trip, became worse and died. Three other children were seriously ill. We had been floating for about an hour when the United States Coast Guard found us. The men who boarded our boat looked like the pictures of the mercenaries[6] I had seen in my reading book at school. I was surprised that these men took great care in evacuating the sick people and then gave the rest of us fruit to eat. Then they took us aboard their ship. My grandfather, brother, father and I were taken to the captain's quarters where we ate soup. All of us began to feel somewhat better.

"When we arrived in Key West, we were interviewed and taken to a dining area. Since my brother and I had lost our shoes in Cuba, we had to go barefoot. We were given good food to eat and a place to rest. The next morning we had breakfast and then boarded a large airplane for a military camp in Pennsylvania.

"The weather at the camp was cold. My brother and I still had no shoes. At this camp we ate military fashion, out of a can. Even though the style of food was different, the food was good. We took showers and then were taken to a large building where we were asked a lot of questions such as our birthdate and grade in school. They took our pictures and fingerprints. We were given identification cards and meal tickets. My brother and I were given some shoes. The whole family was issued mattresses, sheets, pillows. We slept until daybreak the next day.

"That first day we did not realize that we would be learning a new way of life that was to become a habit for us for the next 40 days. Although the food at the camp was good, we had to wait in long lines. As I watched the Cubans inside the fenced area and the Americans on the

---

6. **mercenaries** (MER-suh-nehr-eez) *n. pl.* soldiers serving in a foreign country for pay

outside, I realized that Cubans were different from North Americans. It was difficult for us to wait in long lines. We did not like to be restrained. Every day that passed at this camp seemed to be worse. Often the women fought and made life difficult for everyone. When we were given new clothing, some of these women would try to see who could get the most. . . .

"As my birthday approached, I began to miss my home and my country more and more. I constantly thought about my family in Cuba and about my school, the teachers and the students there. Each day that passed made my life at this cold regimented camp more unbearable. On the day of my birthday I really felt depressed. The day started off badly for me. For breakfast I was unable to eat because all the women crowded in front of me. Some of them got seconds before I was able to get anything. I became discouraged and completely fed up with life at this camp. With all that we had suffered since we decided to leave Cuba, here we were in this military prison and couldn't even get a plate of food for breakfast. In Cuba always on my birthday I received at least one small gift. All of the family, my grandparents, uncles and aunts, cousins and friends came over to celebrate. When I thought about all these people who were so close to me, I began to feel as though I would never be able to go on with life. Separated from all that was familiar to me and unable to go to school, I completely lost my temper and shouted at my mother. I called her some very bad names and blamed her for causing us to abandon our country. I believed it was her fault that we were in this mess. This was truly the saddest day of my life.

"A few weeks later after a great deal of effort we were able to locate a sponsor, a Cuban doctor who had left the country years ago. He and his family lived in Michigan. They agreed to come and get us from the camp. It was a 12 hour trip from their home in Michigan to the camp in

Pennsylvania. They came to pick us up in their motor home. None of us had ever seen such a vehicle. On the way back to Michigan the family told us all about their town, their home and their life in the United States. The children described some of the places they planned to take us. One place was especially interesting to my brother and me. It was a large park with many rides. They said that once we were in the park, we could go on each ride as many times as we wanted. All of the places they described sounded incredible to us. We wanted to know and to do everything. By coincidence, the day we left for Michigan was Independence Day, the Fourth of July. We saw a lot of fireworks that night as we drove along the highway to Michigan. I did not really understand what they meant, but I hoped that I would learn soon.

"When we arrived at our friend's house in Michigan, my brother and I could hardly believe it was possible our friends lived in such a house. It had 6 bedrooms, 2 bathrooms, and a huge basement. It was located on 5 acres of land. There were many different kinds of animals that lived on the farmland around the house. My grandfather immediately decided that he would be in charge of taking care of the animals. My grandmother volunteered to take care of everything in the kitchen. My father got a job as a welder and my mother started to work in our doctor friend's office. Today my brother and I enroll in a new school where we will get to know students who speak another language and who will, I hope, in the not too distant future, become our new friends."

AFTER YOU READ

Exchanging Backgrounds and Cultures

1. Recall the difficulties the author's family had to face during the immigration process. What does this process tell you about the Cuban government's attitude toward Cubans who wanted to leave the country?

2. In what ways does the author say that Cubans are different from North Americans?

3. The family's sponsor also came to the United States from Cuba, but some years earlier. Why might this be an advantage to the family?

What Do You Think?

Which image or event in this diary caught your interest most? Why was this image or event especially meaningful to you?

Experiencing Nonfiction

In his diary, the author tells about activities at his school in Cuba. How is your school like or different from the Cuban school? What kinds of school activities do you take part in on a daily basis? Write a diary entry that describes a day at your school.

Optional Activity The author remembers what his birthday celebration in Cuba was like. He might have called it "the happiest day of my life." Write a diary entry about a birthday celebration—yours or someone else's—and tell why it stands out in your memory. Focus on the feelings surrounding this particular occasion, such as anticipation, surprise, frustration, or joy.

INTRODUCTION
Little Things Are Big

Jesus Colon (heh-SOOS koh-LOHN) came to the United States from Cayey, Puerto Rico, in 1918. He was 17 years old at the time. Colon was part of a wave of Puerto Rican workers, many of them trained cigar makers, who came to find work in New York City.

While in Puerto Rico, Colon was concerned about the way that workers were treated and the unfair conditions under which they worked. He began writing, in part, to help make the general public aware of workers' problems. His writing appeared in newspapers in both Puerto Rico and New York City.

Colon, who died in 1974, left a valuable record of what life was like for the early Puerto Rican immigrants to the United States. Some of his writings, in the form of autobiographical accounts, fictional pieces, and articles, appear in the book *A Puerto Rican in New York*. The selection you are about to read, "Little Things Are Big," is about an incident that left Colon feeling that he had failed himself.

Little Things Are Big

by Jesus Colon

It was very late at night on the eve of Memorial Day. She came into the subway at the 34th Street Pennsylvania Station. I am still trying to remember how she managed to push herself in with a baby on her right arm, a valise in her left hand and two children, a boy and girl about three and five years old, trailing after her. She was a nice looking white lady in her early twenties.

At Nevins Street, Brooklyn, we saw her preparing to get off at the next station—Atlantic Avenue—which happened to be the place where I too had to get off. Just as it was a problem for her to get on, it was going to be a problem for her to get off the subway with two small children to be taken care of, a baby on her right arm and a medium sized valise in her left hand.

And there I was, also preparing to get off at Atlantic Avenue, with no bundles to take care of—not even the customary book under my arm without which I feel that I am not completely dressed.

As the train was entering the Atlantic Avenue station, some white man stood up from his seat and helped her out, placing the children on the long, deserted platform. There were only two adult persons on the long platform some time after midnight on the eve of last Memorial Day.

I could perceive the steep, long concrete stairs going down to the Long Island Railroad or into the street. Should I offer my help as the American white man did at the subway door placing the two children outside the subway car? Should I take care of the girl and the boy, take them by their hands until they reached the end of the steep long concrete stairs of the Atlantic Avenue station?

Courtesy is a characteristic of the Puerto Rican. And here I was—a Puerto Rican—hours past midnight, a valise, two white children and a white lady with a baby on her arm palpably needing somebody to help her at least until she descended the long concrete stairs.

But how could I, a Negro and a Puerto Rican approach this white lady who very likely might have preconceived prejudices against Negroes and everybody with foreign accents, in a deserted subway station very late at night?

What would she say? What would be the first reaction of this white American woman, perhaps coming from a small town with a valise, two children and a baby on her right arm? Would she say: Yes, of course, you may help me. Or would she think that I was just trying to get too familiar? Or would she think worse than that perhaps? What would I do if she let out a scream as I went toward her to offer my help?

Was I misjudging her? So many slanders are written every day in the daily press against the Negroes and Puerto Ricans. I hesitated for a long, long minute. The ancestral manners that the most illiterate Puerto Rican passes on from father to son were struggling inside me. Here was I, way past midnight, face to face with a situation that could very well explode into an outburst of prejudices and chauvinistic conditioning of the "divide and rule" policy of present day society.

It was a long minute. I passed on by her as if I saw

nothing. As if I was insensitive to her need. Like a rude animal walking on two legs, I just moved on half running by the long subway platform leaving the children and the valise and her with the baby on her arm. I took the steps of the long concrete stairs in twos until I reached the street above and the cold air slapped my warm face.

This is what racism and prejudice and chauvinism and official artificial divisions can do to people and to a nation!

Perhaps the lady was not prejudiced after all. Or not prejudiced enough to scream at the coming of a Negro toward her in a solitary subway station a few hours past midnight.

If you were not that prejudiced, I failed you, dear lady. I know that there is a chance in a million that you will read these lines. I am willing to take that millionth chance. If you were not that prejudiced, I failed you, lady, I failed you, children. I failed myself to myself.

I buried my courtesy early on Memorial Day morning. But here is a promise I make to myself here and now; if I am ever faced with an occasion like that again, I am going to offer my help regardless of how the offer is going to be received.

Then I will have my courtesy with me again.

AFTER YOU READ

Exchanging Backgrounds and Cultures

1. Why does Colon fear the woman will react negatively if he offers to help her? What does this reveal about the society of the time?

2. What does this essay suggest about Colon's feelings about himself as both black and Latino?

3. How does Colon's feeling that he has failed himself show how he feels about his heritage? How is this attitude reflected in the promise he makes to himself?

What Do You Think?

Which part of this essay is especially meaningful to you? Why is it important?

Experiencing Nonfiction

In this essay, Colon describes an event that left him feeling as though he had failed himself. The event made him determined to behave differently in the future. Think about an experience you have had that made you feel determined to react differently to similar situations in the future. Write an essay in which you tell the lesson you learned from the experience.

Optional Activity Assume that Colon is able to keep his promise to himself. Write an essay—or a new ending for the essay "Little Things Are Big"—as if you were Colon. In your essay, tell about how you offer help and how your offer is received. Remember to use the first-person pronoun *I* in your writing.

INTRODUCTION

El Doctor

Born in the Dominican Republic in 1950, Julia Alvarez (HOOL-yah AHL-vah-res) came to the United States with her family when she was 10 years old. A published essayist, poet, and writer of fiction, Alvarez has won several prizes. After receiving degrees in literature and creative writing, she taught poetry in schools in Kentucky, California, Vermont, Washington, D.C., and Illinois. In an international competition held in 1988, Alvarez was chosen one of five artists to live and work as a Resident Writer in Altos de Chavón, an artist colony in the Dominican Republic. Alvarez is currently a teacher at Middlebury College in Vermont, where she teaches a course about Latino writers in the United States.

In the following biographical sketch, "El Doctor," Alvarez tells about life with her father. Her portrait of him shows that despite his success in the United States, part of him still reflects his Dominican childhood when he was always afraid that "the good things would run out." An immigrant herself, Alvarez is sensitive to being part of both worlds.

El Doctor

by Julia Alvarez

"Lights! At this hour?" my father asks, looking up from his empty dinner plate at the glowing lamp my mother has just turned on above the table. "Are we in Plato's cave,[1] Mother?" He winks at me; as the two readers in the family we show off by making allusions my mother and sisters don't understand. He leans his chair back and picks up the hem of the curtain. A dim gray light falls into the room. "See, Mother. It's still light out there!"

"*Ya, ya!*" she snaps, and flips the switch off.

"Your mother is a wonder," he announces, then he adds, "El Doctor is ready for bed." Dinner is over; every night my father brings the meal to a close with a third-person goodnight before he leaves the room.

Tonight he lingers, watching her. She says nothing, head bent, intent on her mashed plantains with oil and onions. "Yessir," he elaborates, "El Doctor—" The rest is garbled, for he's balled up his napkin and rubbed his lips

---

1. **Plato's cave** (PLAY-tohs KAYV) In "Allegory of the Cave," the Greek philosopher Plato compares our search for meaning in life to leaving a safe, dark, but happy cave to enter the burning light of the sun of truth.

violently as if he meant to erase them from his face. Perhaps he shouldn't have spoken up? She is jabbing at the few bites of beefsteak on her plate. Perhaps he should have just let the issue drop like water down his chest or whatever it is the Americans say. He scrapes his chair back.

Her scowl deepens. "Eduardo, please." And then, because he already knows better, she adds only, "The wax finish."

"*Por supuesto,*"[2] he says, his voice full of false concern as he examines her spotless kitchen floor for damages. Then, carefully, he lifts his chair up and tucks it back in its place. "This old man is ready for bed." He leans over and kisses the scowl off her face. "Mother, this country agrees with you. You look more beautiful every day. Doesn't she, girls?" And with a wink of encouragement to each of us, he leave us in the dark.

I remember my mother mornings, slapping around in her comfortable slippers, polishing her windows into blinding panes of light. But I remember him mostly at night, moving down the dark halls, undressing as he climbed the dark stairs to bed.

I want to say there were as many buttons on his vest as stairs up to the bedroom: it seemed he unbuttoned a button on each step so that by the time he reached the landing, his vest was off. His armor, I thought, secretly pleased with all I believed I understood about him. But his vest couldn't have had more than six buttons, and the stairs were long and narrow. Of course, I couldn't see well in the dark he insisted on.

"I'm going to take this dollar," he showed me, holding a bill in one hand and a flickering lighter in the other, "and I'm going to set fire to it." He never actually did. He spoke in parables, he complained in metaphor because he

---

2. *Por supuesto* (pawr soo-PWEH-stoh) of course

had never learned to say things directly. I already knew what he meant, but I had my part to play.

"Why would you want to do something like that?" I asked.

"Exactly! Why burn up my money with all these lights in the house!" As we grew up, confirmed in our pyromania,[3] he did not bother to teach us to economize, but went through the house, turning off lights in every room, not noticing many times that we were there, reading or writing a letter, and leaving us in the dark, hurt that he had overlooked us.

At the bedroom door he loosened his tie and, craning his neck, undid the top button of his shirt. Then he sat at the edge of the bed and turned on his bedside lamp. Not always; if a little reflected sun dappled the room with shadowy light, if it was late spring or early fall or summertime, he waited until the last moment to turn on the lamp, sometimes reading in the dark until we came in and turned it on for him. "Papi, you're going to ruin your eyes," we scolded.

Once I worked it out for him with the pamphlet the electric company sent me. Were he to leave his bedside light, say, burning for the rest of his evenings—and I allowed him a generous four decades ("I won't need it for that long," he protested; I insisted)—the cost (side by side we multiplied, added, carried over to the next column) would be far less than if he lost his eyesight, was forced to give up his practice and had to spend the next four decades—

"Like your friend Milton,"[4] he said, pleased with the inspired possibilities of blindness." Now that I was turning

---

3. **pyromania** (py-ruh-MAY-nee-uh) *n.* a mental condition in which a person has strong urges to set fires
4. **Milton** (MIHL-tuhn) (1608–1674) refers to John Milton, an English poet who became blind

out to be the family poet, all the greats were my personal friends. "'When I considered how my light is spent,'" he began. He loved to recite, racing me through poems to see who would be the first one to finish.

"'How my light is spent,'" I echoed and took the lead. "'Ere half my days, in this dark world and wide . . .'"

Just as I was rounding the linebreak to the last line, he interjected it, "'They also serve who only stand and wait.'"

I scowled. How dare he clap the last line on after I had gone through all the trouble of reciting the poem! "Not every blind man is a Milton," I said, and I gave him the smirk I wore all through adolescence.

"Nutrition," he said mysteriously.

"What about nutrition?"

"Good nutrition, we're starting to see the effects: children grow taller; they have better teeth, better bones, better minds than their elders." And he reached for his book on the bedside table.

Actually, the reading came later. First there is the scene that labels him immigrant and shows why I could never call him, sweetly, playfully, *Daddy*. He took from his back pocket a wad of bills so big his hand could not close over it. And he began to count. If at this point we disturbed him, he waved us away. If we called from downstairs, he did not answer. All over the bed he shared with my mother were piles of bills: I do not know the system; no one ever did. Perhaps all the fives were together, all the tens? Perhaps each pile was a specific amount? But this was the one private moment he insisted on. Not even catching him undressing, which I never did, seems as intimate a glimpse of him.

After the counting came the binding and marking: each pile was held together with rubber bands he saved from the rolled-up *New York Times,* and the top bill was scribbled on. He marked them as a reminder of how much was in each pile, I'm sure, but I can't help thinking it was also his way of owning what he had earned, much as ranchers brand their cattle.

The Secretary of the Treasury had signed this twenty; there was Andrew Jackson's picture; he had to add his hand to it to make it his—to try to convince himself that it was his, for he never totally believed it was. Even after he was a successful doctor in New York with a house in the suburbs and lands at "home," his daughters in boarding schools and summer camps, a second car with enough gadgets to keep him busy in bad traffic, he was turning off lights, frequenting thrift shops for finds in ties, taking the 59th Street bridge even if it was out of his way to avoid paying a toll to cross the river.

He could not afford the good life, he could only pass it on. And he did. Beneath the surface pennypinching, his extravagance might have led him to bankruptcy several times had mother not been there to remind him that the weather was apt to change. "Save for a snowy day," she advised him.

"Julie! Isn't it rainy day?" he enlisted me. He was always happy to catch his wife at an error since she spoke English so much better than he did. "Save it for a rainy day?"

Eager to be an authority on anything, I considered Arbiter[5] of Clichés a compliment to my literary talent. "Save it for a rainy day," I agreed.

"See, Mother."

She defended herself. "Snow is much worse than rain.

---

5. Arbiter (AHR-bih-ter) *n.* a person chosen to settle a dispute

For one thing, you need to own more clothes in the winter . . ."

Out from his pocket came a ten when we needed small change for the subway. Away at college I opened the envelope, empty but for the money order for fifty, a hundred; typed out in the blank beside *for* was his memo: "Get yourself a little something in my name." It was the sixties and parental money was under heavy suspicion; my friends needed me as a third world person to be a good example of poverty and oppression by the capitalist, military-industrial complex. I put my little somethings quietly in the bank. By the time I graduated from college, I had a small corrupt fortune.

But my rich father lived in the dark, saving string, going the long way. I've analyzed it with my economist friends. Perhaps since his fortune came from the same work which in his country had never earned him enough, he could never believe that his being well-to-do wasn't an I.R.S. oversight. My psychologist friends claim that it is significant that he was the youngest of twenty-five children. Coming after so many, he would always fear that the good things would run out. And indeed he had a taste for leftovers, which made his compliments come a day or two after a special meal. Whenever we had chicken, he insisted on the wings and the neck bone because those had been the portions left by the time the platter got to him, the baby. He liked the pale, bitter center of the lettuce. ("The leaves were gone when I got the salad bowl.") And when we had soup, he was surprised to find a piece of meat bobbing at the surface. "Someone missed this one."

Unlike mother, he saved for a sunny day. Extravaganza! On his birthday, on Christmas, on his saint's day which was never celebrated for anyone else, his presents multiplied before us. Beside the ones we had bought for him, there were always other glossy packages, ribboned boxes which dwarfed ours. The cards were forged: "To my dearest father from his loving daughter," "Which of you gave me this?" he asked with mock surprise and real delight. Cordelias[6] all, we shook our heads as he unwrapped a silk lounging jacket or a genuine leather passport case. I wish he had allowed someone to give him something.

Perhaps we did on those evenings after the money was counted and put away, and he was ready for company. With an instinct for his rituals, we knew when it was time to come into the bedroom. We heard the bathroom door click shut; he was undressing, putting on his pajamas. The hamper lid clapped on its felt lip. We heard steps. The bed creaked. We found him in the darkening room with a book. "Papi, you're ruining your eyes!" and we turned on the bedside lamp for him since he could not give himself the luxury of that light. "Oh my God, it's gotten dark already," he almost thanked us.

He wanted company, not conversation. He had us turn on the television so we could learn our English. This after years here, after his money had paid for the good private schools which unrolled our r's and softened our accents; after American boyfriends had whispered sweet colloquialisms[7] in our ears. As the television's cowboys and beauty queens and ladies with disappointing stains in their wash droned on in their native English, he read the usual:

---

6. **Cordelia** (kawr-DEEL-yuh) in Shakespeare's play *King Lear*, the only daughter of the king who is truly devoted to him
7. **colloquialisms** (kuh-LOH-kwee-uhl-ihz-uhmz) *n. pl.* words or phrases used in conversation but not in formal speech or writing

a history book in Spanish. We sat at the edge of the king-size bed and wondered what he wanted from us. He wanted presences: Walter Cronkite, his children, his wife, the great gods of the past, Napoleon, Caesar, Maximilian.[8] If one of us, bored with his idea of company, got up to leave, he lowered his book. "Did you know that in the campaign of 1808, Napoleon left his General behind to cut off the enemy from the rear, and the two divisions totally missed each other?" That was the only way he knew to ask us to stay, appealing to history and defeat, to wintry campaigns, bloody frost-bitten feet, a field strewn with war dead.

I taste the mints that he gave us, one each. He kept a stash of them in a drawer next to his bed like a schoolboy and ate exactly one each night and gave away four. That was the other way he kept us there if we got up to go after Napoleon's troops had been annihilated. "Don't you want a mint?" He didn't mean right then and there. It was a promise we had to wait for, perhaps until the chapter ended or the Roman empire fell or he was sure we had given up on the evening and decided to stay, talking in code with each other about school, our friends, our wild (for that room) adventures.

We were not fooled into rash confessions there, for at the merest hint of misadventure, the book came down like a coffin lid on Caesar or Claudius.[9] Oh, we confessed, we were just exaggerating! Of course we didn't raid the dorm

---

8. **Napoleon** (nuh-POHL-yuhn) Napoleon Bonaparte (1769–1821) a great general and emperor of France from 1804 to 1815; **Caesar** (SEE-zer) Gaius Julius Caesar (100–44 B.C.) Roman general, statesman, and writer; **Maximilian** (mak-suh-MIHL-yuhn) emperor of Mexico from 1864 to 1867
9. **Claudius** (KLAWD-ee-uhs) Tiberius Claudius Drusus Nero Germanicus (10 B.C.–A.D. 54) emperor of Rome from A.D. 41 to 54

kitchen at midnight, our friends did. "Tell me who your friends are," he said in Spanish, "and I'll tell you who *you* are." No, we hadn't gotten help on our math. "The man who reaches the summit following another's trail will not find his way back to his own valley." If he caught us, hurrying, scurrying, here, there, he stopped us mid-flight to tell us what Napoleon had said to his valet, "Dress me slowly, I'm in a hurry."

But why look beyond one's own blood for good examples? "You come from good stock," he bragged when I came home from boarding school, my pride wounded. I'd been called ugly names by some great-great-granddaughters of the American Revolution. "You tell them your great-grandfather was the son of a count." . . .

"You don't understand, you don't understand," I wailed, hot tears welling in my eyes. And I closed the door of my room, forbidding anyone to enter.

"What's she doing in there, Mother?" I heard him ask her.

"I don't know. Writing poetry or something."

"Are you sure? You think she's all right?". . .

"These girls are going to drive us crazy!" My mother said. "That's what I'm sure of. One of them has to have straight hair. Straight hair, at this stage of the game! Another wants to spend the weekend at a boy's school. All the other girls get to! This one wants to die young and miserable!" Then she yelled at father. "I'm going to end up in Bellevue![10] And then you're all going to be very sorry!" I heard the rushed steps down the stairs, the bang of the screen door, finally the patter of the hose as she watered the obedient grass in the growing dark.

He knocked first, "Hello?" he asked tentatively, the

---

10. **Bellevue** (BEL-vyoo) *n.* medical center in New York City with a well-known psychiatric facility

door ajar. "Hello, hello, Edgar Allan Poe," he teased, entering. He sat at the foot of my bed and told me the story of his life.

"The point is," he concluded, "*'La vida es sueño y los sueños, sueños son.'*"[11] He stood by the window and watched my mother watering her fussy bushes as if she could flush roses out of them. "My father," he turned to me, "used to say that to my mother: Life is a dream, Mauran, and dreams are dreams."

He came across the shadowy room as if he did not want anyone to overhear. It was getting late. In the darkening garden she would be winding the hose into drooping coils. "Always, always," he said. "I always wanted to be a poet. *'La vida es sueño,'* 'They also serve who only stand and wait.' 'To be or not to be.' Can you imagine! To say such things! My God! Everyone gets a little something." He cupped his hands towards me. I nodded, too stunned at his flood of words to ask him what he meant. "And some make a building," he made a building with a wave of his hand. "Some," he rubbed his thumb and index finger together, "make money. Some make friends, connections, you know. But some, some make something that can change the thinking of mankind! Oh my God!" He smacked his forehead with his palm in disbelief. "Think of the Bible. Think of your friend Edgar Allan Poe. But then," he mused, "then you grow older, you discover . . ." He looked down at me. I don't know what he saw in my eyes, perhaps how young I still was, perhaps his eyes duplicated in my face. He stopped himself.

"You discover?" I said.

---

11. *La vida es sueño y los sueños, sueños son* (lah VEE-dah ehs SWEH-nyoh ee lohs SWEH-nyohs SWEH-nyohs sohn) from *Life Is a Dream* by the Spanish playwright Calderón (1600–1681)

But he was already half way across the room. "Papi?" I tried to call him back.

"Your mother," he explained, letting himself out of the room and the revelation. "I think she is calling for me."

A few days later as I sat in his bedroom after supper, waiting for him to fall asleep, I tried to get him to finish his sentence. He couldn't remember what he was about to say, he said, but speaking of discoveries, "We're descended from the conquistadores,[12] you know? Your grandfather traveled the whole north coast[13] on horseback! Now there was a great man!". . .

His mother? He sighed. Don't talk to him about his mother! A saint! Sweet, very religious, patience personified, always smiling. They didn't make them like that anymore, with a few exceptions, he winked at me. . . .

"Does mother remind you of her?" I asked, thinking that leading questions might help him remember what he had been about to say in my room a few nights ago.

"Your mother is a wonder," he said. A good woman, so devoted, so thorough, a little nervous, so giving, a little forceful, a good companion, a little too used to her own way, so generous. "Every garland needs a few thorns," he added.

"I heard that," she said, coming into the room, "What was that about too used to my own way?"

"Did I say that, girls?" father turned to us. "No, Mami, you misheard."

"Then what did you say?"

"What did I say, girls?"

---

12. **conquistadores** (kohn-kees-tah-DOHR-es) *n. pl.* any of the Spanish conquerors of Mexico and Peru in the 16th century
13. **north coast** (NAWRTH KOHST) the north coast of the Caribbean island of Hispaniola

We shrugged, leaving him wide open.

"I said, Mother," he said, unwrapping a rare second mint and putting it in his mouth to buy time. "I said: so used to giving to others. Mother, you're too generous!"

"Ay, put gravy on the chicken." She waved him off, terribly pleased as father winked at our knowing looks.

A few nights later, still on the track of his secret self, I asked him, "Papi, how do you see yourself?" Only I, who had achieved a mild reputation as a deep thinker, could get away with such questions.

"You ask deep questions," he mused, interrupting Napoleon's advance across the Russian steppes.[14] "I like that."

He offered me my mint and unwrapped his. "I am the rock," he said, nodding.

"Ay, Papi, that's too impersonal. How do you perceive yourself. What kind of man are you?" I was young and thought such definitions could be given and trusted. I was young and ready to tear loose, but making it harder for myself by trying to understand those I was about to wound.

"I am a rock," he repeated, liking his analogy. "Mother, you girls, my sisters, everyone needs my support. I am the strong one!". . .

"But, Papi," I whispered as I moved from the armchair to the foot of his bed, "you don't always have to be strong."

That was my mistake. The conversation was over. He hated touching scenes; they confused him. Perhaps as the last child of an older, disappointed woman, he was used to diffuse attention, not intimacy. To take hold of a hand, to graze a cheek and whisper an endearment were beyond him. Tenderness had to be mothered by necessity: he was a

---

14. steppes (STEHPS) *n. pl.* vast, treeless plains

good doctor. Under the cover of Hippocrates'[15] oath, with the stethoscope around his neck and the bright examination light flushing out the personal and making any interchange terribly professional, he was amazingly delicate: tapping a bone as if it were the fontanelle[16] of a baby, easing a patient back on a pillow like a lover his sleeping beloved, stroking hair away from a feverish forehead. But now he turned away.

He fell asleep secretly in that room full of presences, my mother beside him. No one knew exactly when it happened. We looked to him during a commercial or when a slip had implicated us in some forbidden adventure, and the book had collapsed like a card house on his chest and his glasses rode the bridge of his nose like a schoolmarm's. Though if we got up to leave and one of us reached for his glasses he woke with a start. "I'm not asleep!" he lied. "Don't go yet. It's early."

He fell asleep in the middle of the Hundred Days while Napoleon marched towards Waterloo[17] or, defeated, was shipped off to St. Helena.[18] We stifled our giggles at his comic-book snores, the sheets pulled over his head, his nose poking out like a periscope. Very quietly, widening our eyes at each other as if that might stop any noise, we rose. One turned off the set and threw a kiss at mother, who put her finger to her lips from her far side of the bed.

---

15. **Hippocrates** (hihp-AHK-ruh-teez) a Greek physician who lived from about 460 to 377 B.C. and is often called the "father of medicine"; he is credited with providing an ideal of ethics and professional conduct for physicians through the Hippocratic Oath

16. **fontanelle** (fahn-tuh-NEHL) *n.* membrane-covered opening in an infant's skull

17. **Waterloo** (wawt-er-LOO) town in Belgium near the site of a battle in 1815 at which Napoleon was defeated

18. **Saint Helena** (SAYNT huh-LEE-nuh) an island in the South Atlantic where Napoleon lived in exile following his defeat at Waterloo

Another and another kiss traveled across the hushed room.
A scolding wave from mother hurried my sisters out.

I liked to be the one who stayed, bending over the
bedside table strewn with candy wrappers, slipping a hand
under the tassled shade. I turned the switch over, once.
The room burst into brighter light, the tassels swung
madly, mother signaled to me, crossly, Out! Out at once! I
shrugged apologies. Her scowl deepened. Father groaned.
I bent closer. I turned again. The room went back into
economical dark.

AFTER YOU READ

Exchanging Backgrounds and Cultures

1. Dr. Alvarez was the youngest of 25 children in a poor family living in a troubled nation. How did this affect his behavior and attitude?

2. In what parts of Dr. Alvarez's past does he seem to take the most pride?

3. Dr. Alvarez tries to comfort his daughter about her unpleasant experiences in boarding school by bringing up their family background. Why do you think he does this? Why do his efforts seem to fail?

What Do You Think?

Which part of this biographical sketch is most meaningful to you? Why did it stand out?

Experiencing Nonfiction

In this sketch, Alvarez describes conversations and incidents with her father that show that she and he share a special bond. Think about a favorite person of yours. Write a biographical sketch that shows how this person is important to you.

Optional Activity Write a biographical sketch of an older relative or friend. Like Alvarez, who reveals her father's interests, describe this person's interests and ideas.

INTRODUCTION
La Luisa

Pablo Medina (PAH-bloh meh-DEE-nah) was born in Cuba and left there with his family when he was 12 years old. He has lived in the United States since 1960. His poetry, prose, and translations of the work of other Latino writers have appeared in many magazines and collections. Medina teaches English and Spanish at Mercer County Community College in Trenton, New Jersey.

The selection you are about to read, "La Luisa," is from Medina's book *Exiled Memories: A Cuban Childhood*. In this autobiographical account, Medina gives some of the history of Cuban *colonias*, or farms, and shares his memories of childhood vacations on his grandfather's colonia. The setting of his personal memoir is pre-revolutionary Cuba. Medina brings to life the Cuba of his past. He shows what Cuban life was like before the years of change that occurred under Fidel Castro.

La Luisa
from *Exiled Memories: A Cuban Childhood*
by Pablo Medina

Cuba has a province named Matanzas, after a series of slaughters perpetrated by Spanish soldiers on the Indians of the area. The province, east of Havana, stretches toward the center of the island and is considered to be among the most fertile. Endless fields of sugarcane, interrupted occasionally by sugar mills and towns, simmer in the sun like green fire. To the south, hills and valleys meld into what is referred to by geographers as the Llanura Roja[1] (the Red Plain). The ground there is blood red. Toward the lower edge of the Llanura my grandfather had his *colonia,* La Luisa.

An interesting term, *colonia.* It is derived directly from the Latin word meaning farm or settlement; but in Cuba it was a throwback to the period after the Ten Years' War (1868–1878), when, with the end of slavery, sugar mills were forced to parcel out their landholdings to sugar farmers called *colonos.*[2] At first the *colonos* were little more than indentured farmers, having to give the sugar mill a substantial portion of their harvest. With time, however,

---

1. **Llanura Roja** (yah-NOO-rah ROH-hah)
2. *colonos* (koh-LOH-nohs)

the *colonos* thrived on the land, and eventually their descendants identified more with the island that gave them birth than with the distant Spanish lion. Out of this homegrown race, the creoles,[3] came many revolutionaries who helped liberate the country from the grip of monarchy and colonialism. This same revolutionary tradition, born out of the creoles' need to find an identity as a people, crested in 1959 when the word *colonia* at last became an archaism in the fullest sense. Farms in Cuba are now known as "agricultural cooperatives."

La Luisa lay between two towns on the southern circuit of the Carretera Central, the main highway that ran the length of the island. In the north was Pedro Betancourt, formerly known as Corral Falso, where my grandparents had their townhouse; to the south, beyond Jardines, a *colonia* owned by my great-uncle Octavio and his countless sons, was a smaller town, Torrientes. Farther east and south was Jagüey Grande, the last town before Zapata Swamp, a vast area bare of human habitation but for the shacks of the *carboneros*[4] (charcoal makers), semiwild people who eked out a living by selling charcoal to nearby farmers.

I would spend summers and winter vacations at the *colonia*. When my parents couldn't drive me, they would send me in a *botero*,[5] a collective taxi that followed the route from Havana to Pedro Betancourt. One of my earliest memories is one of these rides. Besides myself and the driver Zacarías, there was a black family of five who were on their way to visit relatives in the country. The only

---

3. **creoles** (KREE-ohlz) *n. pl.* persons of European descent born in the West Indies or Latin America
4. *carboneros* (kahr-boh-NEH-rohs)
5. *botero* (boh-TEH-roh)

one of them who stands out clearly in my mind now is the patriarch.[6] He wore a white guayabera[7] and white pants that contrasted sharply with his coal black skin. He was wrinkled, very wrinkled, as if the river of life had once flowed through him and now only its dried-out imprint remained, and he smelled of molasses and lime. . . .

Once a large front garden with many flowering bushes stretched from the house to a stone wall by the railroad tracks, but I barely remember that. Eminent domain[8] had been invoked by government engineers and the highway was built right through the garden. Not that my grandparents minded. Getting in and out of La Luisa had been, before the road appeared, a slow and arduous process, and during heavy rain it was impossible, except on horseback. The house itself was a purely functional wood frame structure with floor-to-ceiling windows that allowed the breeze to cool the interior even on the hottest summer afternoon. The floor was concrete slab painted red, making for easy cleaning. In the back, behind the bedrooms that opened railroad style onto an exposed hallway, were the kitchen, a large pantry, and the charcoal storage room. A wooden gate led to the backyard where my world started.

For La Luisa was a place that belonged to the outside: to the animals, the trees, the sugarcane, the fierce sun and the fierce rain, the soft dusk and the soul-quiet evenings where the sounds of the modern world rarely, if ever, intruded. For me, it was a place of learning and experience, the crucible where humans and nature

---

6. **patriarch** (PAY-tree-ahrk) *n.* the father and head of a family
7. **guayabera** (gwy-ah-BEH-rah) *n.* a long shirt worn outside the pants
8. **Eminent domain** (EHM-uh-nuhnt doh-MAYN) a right of a government to take private property for public use

blended, where sweat gave forth fruit, where the wind whinnied, the moon mooed, and owls whooshed through the night; where luck was as much a good cane harvest as getting out of bed in the morning without stepping on a scorpion.

Farmers like my grandfather, Fiquito, were totally dependent on the whims of the outside, living always on the edge. Hard work mattered, but so did luck, fortune, fate, whatever you want to call it. He went out to the fields at six in the morning just before dawn, returned at noon for dinner, and went out again at three until the sun touched the top of the farthest trees. That was time enough to reach home before dark. Routine helped luck along, nursed it, treated it as a member of the family.

Fortune, however, will turn, as a trusted dog will turn and strike its master. A hurricane, an arsonist's fire, or a fall in sugar prices could ruin a man. Nothing to do then but start over, and never mind that luck had turned against you. You were alive, weren't you, and healthy? You still had a family; you still had the land, rich and red and ready. Above all, you had yourself, for you were the land. It was your birth, your growth, and your death.

Not to realize this was to be no man on the earth, bound to fail as a *colono.* If he ever taught me anything, Fiquito showed me in his life that no one is any better than anyone else; it is just that good fortune like good rain will fall in one spot and not another and may stop as suddenly as it comes.

My grandfather, true farmer that he was, loved the land not in a patriotic sense, but rather as a son. Thus, his unquestioning devotion to it and his confidence when working it. Fiquito could know no other life because he knew no other place. His country was the earth and he dealt not with principles and ideals but with planting and harvesting and the ever present cycle of life and death. In retrospect, all of us who knew him are relieved that he died one year before the Castro take-over. Not that the land would have been taken from him as it was taken from grandfather Mina, but he would have been taken from the land, losing that vital connection to existence that made him admirable as a person. Better off dead of cancer than to have had the hurricane of fate pull him up by his roots and fling him to a netherworld of concrete, artificial lights, and hands that grasp at empty air for something to hold on to and find not even their own shadows. Even in his final delirium, Fiquito talked of the land, urging his son-in-law to saddle his horse and unlock the gate so he could leave without delay. He died a lucky man.

La Luisa was a primitive place. It wasn't until the mid-fifties that my grandfather bought his first electric generator. Before then, gaslight and kerosene lamps were the only sources of light at night. Evenings after supper, we would sit on the front porch under the dim flicker of the gas burner, talking, watching the absolute darkness that surrounded our bubble of light. I remember the soft buzz of the flame and the faint sulfurous smell. At around ten o'clock, the two pellets dropped into the canister that fed the system gave out and we all went to bed.

Cooking was done on a charcoal stove. Fiquito would start the first at five in the morning and make coffee. At five-thirty or six, he came to my bed with a steaming cup. At home, I resented being awakened early; in La Luisa waking was a special treat I looked forward to. Fresh Cuban coffee made from beans grown in the garden and sweetened with raw sugar is a drink excelled by few. When it is offered at first hint of dawn, held by the hand that plucked the beans, spread them out in the sun to dry, and ground them, it is a nectar the gods would envy.

Soon after coffee and his breakfast of a raw egg dropped into a glass of sweet sherry, Fiquito would mount his horse that Domingo the foreman had readied, and the two would head out for a day's work.

Out in the fields, the cane cutters huddled in small groups fingering their razor sharp machetes; the oxcarts that carried the cut cane to the railroad depot were lined single file, and the *carreteros*[9] (teamsters) kept the oxen in line with a mixture of curses and caresses. This was the time when it was light enough for them to inspect their animals for ticks, cuts, bruises, and the fit of their yokes, and they did this with much the same intent attitude one sees in the faces of modern day truck drivers checking their rigs. Once Fiquito and Domingo arrived, the work started. The men gathered along the length of the field to cut and slash at the cane, one stalk at a time. They held the stalk midway up with the left hand, then swung the machete to cut the cane three inches above the ground. They cleared the stalk of chaff, held their machetes head high and somewhat to the left, then swung the cane toward the blade and released it as it was cut in two. The pieces twirled in the air and landed on a mound behind each man. The whole process took two or three seconds. As soon as there was enough cane, the first wagon was loaded and sent off to the depot where the load was transferred to railroad cars for its trip to the sugar mill. After the first hour or so of work, a steady stream of oxcart traffic flowed in and out of the field. It was a noisy undertaking. *Carreteros* screamed at the oxen; the oxen mooed and bellowed, protesting the prods their masters applied to their rumps. The more they protested, the more they were prodded. Domingo's voice, gravelly and tough like a stretched sinew, threw itself at the cane cutters. And under

9. *carreteros* (kah-reh-TEH-rohs)

it all was the constant chomp of the machetes as they bit into the ripe cane.

Fiquito sat proudly on his horse. He paced up and down the line, never raising his voice, watching the *macheteros'*[10] work, directing them this way and that, calling for a break when he thought the men needed it. With white guayabera, jodphurs,[11] handmade riding boots, and a Stetson hat he had bought in the capital, he was the embodiment of the benevolent but firm *caudillo.*[12] To further emphasize his authority, he carried a .38-caliber revolver with an ivory handle. At the time, I did not understand why he always wore it in the field. I never once saw him fire the gun, not even for practice. When I grew older, well after he was dead, I tried to reject men like my grandfather because they represented the exploitation of the poor and downtrodden. But I could never dismiss Fiquito directly. He was kind, well mannered, and as fair a man as I have ever met. He paid well by the standards of the time. He provided housing for his workers and a small plot of land for those with families; when they were sick, he took care of them. But as I said, La Luisa was a primitive place. Violence, especially among the itinerant[13] cane cutters, was commonplace. . . . These men were wild and untutored, and they worked like dogs. They also had short tempers, an understandable trait given the brutal nature of

---

10. *macheteros* (mah-sheh-TEH-rohs) *n. pl.* workers who use machetes
11. **jodphurs** (JAHD-puhrz) *n. pl.* trousers for horseback riding made loose and full above the knees and tight from the knees to the ankles
12. *caudillo* (kow-DEE-yoh) *n.* Spanish or Latin American military dictator or leader
13. **itinerant** (y-TIHN-uhr-uhnt) *adj.* traveling from place to place, especially in connection with some kind of work

their work. Fiquito's attitude and the respect he inspired in many of them kept them with their minds on the cutting. The gun was there just in case. Would he have used it? I do not know. The only thing certain is that he never did. . . .

AFTER YOU READ

Exchanging Backgrounds and Cultures

1. Medina vividly describes his grandfather's great love of the land. How do his descriptions reveal Medina's attitude toward his heritage? How is this attitude shown in the way he views his grandfather?

2. Even though this selection is autobiographical, it is more than just Medina's childhood memories. Why might it also be called informational?

3. After the Cuban Revolution, Medina tried to reject men like his grandfather for their "exploitation of the poor and downtrodden." Why couldn't he reject his grandfather?

What Do You Think?

Which part of this autobiographical account makes the strongest impression on you? What makes it important?

Experiencing Nonfiction

In this selection, Medina paints a vivid word picture of his grandfather's farm—its sights, sounds, and smells. Write a description of a place. Be sure to use sensory words that tell how the place looks, sounds, and smells.

Optional Activity Pretend that you are Fiquito, Medina's grandfather. Write an autobiographical sketch that tells about your life at La Luisa. Use information from the selection in describing your life.

UNIT 1: FOCUS ON WRITING

Nonfiction includes many forms, among them essays, news stories, reports, editorials, biographies, and autobiographies. Although these forms vary in purpose, they are alike in that they tell about real-life events, people, and places. For instance, in his autobiographical essay, Jesus Colon describes an important incident in his life.

Writing Nonfiction

Choose one of the following nonfiction forms: biography, autobiography, diary, or essay. Then, using the following steps, write your own work of nonfiction.

The Writing Process

Good writing requires both time and effort. An effective writer completes a number of stages that together make up the writing process. The stages of the writing process are given below to help guide you through your assignment.

Prewriting

First, decide on the type of nonfiction you will write. Then think about possible topics. Brainstorming topics with a classmate can be helpful. List every idea that comes to mind. Then choose the idea that appeals to you the most.

After you have chosen a topic, ask yourself whether it is too broad for the nonfiction form you selected. If your topic is not narrow enough to be covered in that form, try breaking it down into subtopics. You can then choose one of the subtopics as the focus of your piece.

Next, consider your purpose, audience, and tone. Is your purpose to describe, to explain, or to persuade? For whom are you writing? Is your audience familiar with your topic, or will you have to provide background information? Should your tone be informal or formal?

Once you have determined your purpose, audience, and tone, list details related to your topic. If you are planning to include background information, gather facts about the topic. Be sure to record the sources of all your information.

Next, organize the information and details into an outline. Review your outline to see whether you need to add more specific details or eliminate any that are unimportant or unrelated to your topic.

Drafting and Revising

After you have organized your ideas, begin a first draft. Let your thoughts flow, while keeping in mind your purpose, audience, and tone. Refer to your prewriting notes and outline as you write, but feel free to add new ideas and details that occur to you.

When you are ready to revise your first draft, keep several things in mind. First, be sure that you have presented your topic clearly and logically and that you have included enough facts and details to support it. Next, eliminate any ideas that do not relate directly to your topic. Finally, see whether you have included enough background information. For example, Pablo Medina provides historical information about colonias before describing the one that his grandfather owned.

Proofreading and Publishing

When you have finished revising, carefully proofread your work. Correct any errors in spelling, grammar, punctuation, and capitalization. Then make a neat, final copy of your work.

You may want to share your writing with your family or classmates. You might consider submitting it to your school's newspaper or a literary magazine.

UNIT 2

FICTION OF THE LATINO CARIBBEANS

Fiction is a work of the imagination. It may include descriptions of real events, real places, and real people, but the story it tells springs from the mind of the writer.

All works of fiction tell a different story, but they also share common elements. These shared elements are **setting**, the time and place where the story takes place; **characters**, the people that the story is about; and **plot**, the events that take place in the story. Understanding these common elements will help you get more out of reading fiction.

The two most common forms of fiction are novels and short stories. Novels are long works of fiction, involving complex plots, a variety of settings, and numbers of characters. Short stories are briefer. A few characters may be presented in a single setting, and the focus of the story may be on one conflict or situation in the characters' lives.

The stories in this section will introduce you to a variety of characters, conflicts, and settings. Each story deals with a different aspect of the Latino Caribbean experience. These themes include the adjustments to living in a new country, prejudice, and the struggles of people caught between two cultures.

As you read these selections, think about the themes the authors present and how they use dialogue, action, and description to bring the characters, settings, and events to life.

Pepe Cruz is a self-taught Puerto Rican artist who has been painting since he was 14 years old. His paintings, numbering more than 1,000, include portraits of Puerto Rican heroes and colorful landscapes. This painting, entitled *Aibonito*, shows a scene Cruz remembered from his childhood, complete with buses, animals, and a *bodega*, the Spanish word for "grocery store." Part of the artistic Latino community of the South Bronx in New York City, Cruz is also a carpenter who designs and makes his own decorated picture frames.

INTRODUCTION
An Awakening . . .
Summer 1956

Nicholasa Mohr (nee-koh-LAH-sah MOHR) was born in the Bronx, New York, in 1935, which makes her a second-generation mainland Puerto Rican. Her parents, who were born in Puerto Rico and migrated to the U.S. mainland, are called first-generation mainland Puerto Ricans.

Mohr first worked as a graphic artist, then turned her attention to another craft—writing. Her novels about life in New York City's Puerto Rican community have won many awards.

In the story you are about to read, "An Awakening . . . Summer 1956," Mohr tells about a life-changing event that happens to a young Puerto Rican woman in a small Texas community. The young woman is to spend the summer with the family of her friend Ann, whose invitation to stay with them welcomes her as "another member of the family." With this phrase, the author weaves into the story a bit of Puerto Rican tradition: Not only do families feel close ties with their relatives, but these ties also extend to their close friends. At the end of the story, the close relationship between the two friends helps the main character to deal with the event that changed her life.

An Awakening . . . Summer 1956

by Nicholasa Mohr

The young woman looked out of the window as the greyhound bus sped by the barren, hot, dry Texas landscape. She squinted, clearing her vision against the blazing white sunlight. Occasionally, she could discern small adobe[1] houses clumped together like mushrooms, or a gas station and diner standing alone and remote in the flat terrain. People were not visible. They were hiding, she reasoned, seeking relief indoors in the shade. How different from her native Puerto Rico, where luscious plants, trees and flowers were abundant. Green was the color of that Island, soothing, cool, inviting. And people were seen everywhere, living, working, enjoying the outdoors. All of her life had been spent on her beloved land. For more than a decade she had been in service of the church. Now, this was a new beginning. After all, it had been her choice, her sole decision to leave. At the convent school where she had been safe and loved, they had reluctantly bid her farewell with an open invitation to return. Leaving there had been an essential part of working it all out, she thought, one had to start

---

1. **adobe** (ah-DOH-bee) *adj.* a brick that is dried in the sun rather than in an oven or kiln

somewhere. Still, as she now looked out at all the barrenness before her, she felt a stranger in a foreign land and completely alone.

She was on her way to spend the summer with her good friend Ann. They were going to discuss the several directions in which she might continue to work. After all, she had skills; her degrees in elementary education and a master's in counselling. There was also the opportunity offered her of that scholarship toward a doctorate[2] in Ohio. The need to experience the world independently, without the protection of the church, was far more compelling than her new apprehension of the "unknown."

The young woman checked her wristwatch.

"On time . . ." she whispered, and settled back in her seat.

Her friend Ann was now a social worker with the working poor and the Mexican American community in a small town in rural Texas. The invitation to spend most of this summer with Ann and her family had appealed to the young woman, and she had accepted with gratitude.

"You know you are welcome to stay with us for just as long as you want," Ann had written. "You will be like another member of the family."

The knowledge that she would once more be with her good friend, discussing ideas and planning for the future, just as they had done as co-workers back home, delighted and excited her.

"Clines-Corners . . ." the bus driver announced. The next stop would be hers.

"Now, please wait at the bus depot, don't wander off.

---

2. **doctorate** (DAHK-tuh-riht) *n.* the university degree or status of a doctor

Promise to stay put, in case of a change in schedule, and we will pick you up," Ann had cautioned in her last letter.

"Sentry!" the bus driver shouted as the bus came to a sudden halt. She jumped down and the bus sped off barely missing a sleeping dog that had placed itself comfortably under the shade of a large roadside billboard. The billboard picture promised a cool lakeside ride on a motorboat. . . .

She found herself alone and watched a cloud of dust settle into the landscape as the bus disappeared into the horizon. She approached the depot building where two older Mexican men and a young black man, laborers, sat shaded on a wooden porch, eating lunch. She smiled and waved as she passed them. They nodded in response.

Inside at the ticket booth, a tall man with very pink skin peered out at her from under a dark green sun visor.

"Good day," she cleared her throat. The man nodded and waited. "I was wondering . . . eh, if there was some message for me?"

"What?" he asked.

Feeling self conscious and embarrassed, she repeated her question, adding "I'm sorry, but it is that my English is not too perfect. I am not used to speaking English very often."

"What's your name? I can't know if there's a message for you if I don't know your name." She told him, speaking clearly and spelling each letter with care.

"Nope," he shook his head, "ain't nothing here for nobody by that name." The man turned away and continued his work.

The young woman stood for a moment wondering if her friends had received her wire stating she would arrive several hours earlier than expected. Checking the time she realized it was only twelve thirty. They were not expecting her until five in the late afternoon. She walked to the pay phone and dialed Ann's number. She waited as it rang for almost two full minutes before she replaced the receiver. Disappointed, she approached the clerk again.

"Excuse me, sir . . . can I please leave my luggage for a while? There is not an answer where my friends are living."

The man motioned her to a section of luggage racks.

"Cost you fifty cents for the first three hours, and fifteen cents for each hour after that. Pay when you come back." He handed her a soiled blue ticket.

"Thank you very much. Is there a place for me to get a cold drink? It is very hot . . . and I was riding on the bus a long time."

"There's a Coke machine by the garage, right up the street. Can't miss it."

"Well, I would like a place to sit down. I think I saw a small restaurant up on the main street when I got off the bus."

"Miss, you'd be better off at the Coke machine. Soda's nice and cold. You can come back and drink it in here if you'd like." He looked at the young woman for a moment, nodded, and returned once more to his work.

She watched him somewhat confused and shrugged, then walked out into the hot empty street. Two mangy, flea-bitten mutts streaked with oil spots walked up to her wagging their tails.

"Bueno[3] . . ." she smiled, "you must be my welcoming committee." They followed her as she continued up the main street. The barber shop and the hardware store were both closed. Out to lunch, she said to herself, and a nice siesta[4] . . . now that's sensible.

---

3. **Bueno** (BWEH-noh) *interj.* Good
4. **siesta** (see-EHS-tuh) *n.* in Spain and parts of Latin America, an afternoon nap

Playful shouts and shrieking laughter emanated from a group of Mexican children. They ran jumping and pushing a large metal hoop. She waved at them. Abruptly, they stopped, looking with curiosity and mild interest at this stranger. They glanced at each other and, giggling, quickly began once more to run and play their game. In a moment they were gone, heading into a shaded side street.

The red and white sign above the small store displayed in bold printed letters: NATHANS FOOD AND GROCERIES—EAT IN OR TAKE OUT. On the door a smaller sign read, OPEN. Thankful, she found herself inside, enjoying the coolness and serenity of the small cafe. Two tables set against the wall were empty and except for a man seated at the counter, all the stools were unoccupied. No one else was in sight. She took a counter seat a few stools away from the man. After a minute or two, when no one appeared, the young woman cleared her throat and spoke.

"Pardon me . . . somebody. Please, is somebody here?" She waited and before she could speak again, she heard the man seated at the counter shout:

"ED! Hey Ed, somebody's out here. You got a customer!"

A middle-aged portly man appeared from the back. When he saw the young woman, he stopped short, hesitating. Slowly he walked up to her and silently stared.

"Good day," she said. "How are you?" The man now stood with his arms folded quite still without replying. "Can I please have a Pepsi-Cola." Managing a smile, she continued, "It is very hot outside, but I am sure you know that . . ."

He remained still, keeping his eyes on hers. The young woman glanced around her not quite sure what to do next. Then, she cleared her throat and tried again.

"A Pepsi-Cola, cold if you please . . ."

"Don't have no Pepsi-Colas," he responded loudly.

She looked around and saw a full fountain service, and against the rear wall, boxes filled with Pepsi-Colas.

"What's that?" she asked, confused.

The man gestured at the wall directly behind her. "Can't you read English."

Turning, she saw the sign he had directed her to. In large black letters and posted right next to the door she read:

NO COLOREDS
NO MEXICANS
NO DOGS
WILL BE SERVED ON THESE
PREMISES

All the blood in her body seemed to rush to her head. She felt her tongue thicken and her fingers turn as cold as ice cubes. Another white man's face appeared from the kitchen entrance and behind him stood a very black woman peering nervously over his shoulder.

The silence surrounding her stunned her as she realized at the moment all she was—a woman of dark olive complexion, with jet black hair; she spoke differently from these people. Therefore, she was all those things on that sign. She was also a woman alone before these white men. Jesus and the Virgin Mary . . . what was she supposed to do? Colors flashed and danced before her embracing the angry faces and cold hateful eyes that stared at her daring her to say another word. Anger and fear welled up inside her, and she felt threatened even by the shadows set against the bright sun; they seemed like daggers menacing her very existence. She was going to fight, she was not going to let them cast her aside like an animal. Deeply she inhaled searching for her voice, for her composure, and without warning, she heard herself shouting.

"I WOULD LIKE A PEPSI-COLA, I SAID! AND, I WANT IT NOW . . . RIGHT NOW!!" The words spilled out in loud rasps. She felt her heart lodged in her throat, and swallowed trying to push it back down so that she could breathe once more.

"Can't you read . . . girl?" the man demanded.

"I WANT A PEPSI. DAMN IT . . . NOW!" With more boldness, this time her voice resounded, striking the silence with an explosion. Taking out her change purse she slammed several coins on the counter. "NOW!" she demanded staring at the man. "I'm not leaving until I get my drink."

As the young woman and the middle-aged portly man stared, searching each other's eyes, that moment seemed an eternity to her. All she was, all she would ever be, was here right now at this point in time. And so she stood very still, barely blinking, and concentrated, so that not one muscle in her body moved.

He was the first to move. Shaking his head, he smiled and with slow deliberate steps walked over to the cases by the wall and brought back a bottle of Pepsi-Cola, placing it before her. As she picked up the bottle, she felt the heat of the liquid; it was almost too hot to hold.

"Very well," she said, surprised at the calmness in her voice. "May I please have an opener?"

"Girl . . . we ain't got no openers here. Now you got your damned drink . . . that's it. Get the hell out of here!" He turned, ignoring her, and began to work arranging cups behind the counter.

Her eyes watched him and just for an instant the young woman hesitated before she stood, grabbed the bottle and lifted it high above her bringing it down with tremendous force and smashing it against the counter edge. Like hailstones in a storm, pieces of glass flew in every direction, covering the counter and the space around her. The warm bubbling liquid drenched her. Her heavy breathing sucked in the sweetness of the cola.

"KEEP THE CHANGE!" she shouted. Quickly she slammed the door behind her and once again faced the heat and the empty street.

She walked with her back straight and her head held high.

. . . "CAN'T TREAT YOU PEOPLE LIKE HUMAN BEINGS . . . you no good . . ."

His voice faded as she walked past the main street, the bus depot and the small houses of the town. After what seemed a long enough time, she stopped, quite satisfied she was no longer in that town near that awful hateful man. The highway offered no real shade, and so she turned down a side road. There the countryside seemed gentler, a few trees and bushes offered some relief. A clump of bushes up on a mound of earth surrounded a maple tree that yielded an oasis of cool shade. She climbed up the mound and sat looking about her. She enjoyed the light breeze and the flight of large crows that dotted the sky in the distance. The image of the man and what had happened stirred in her a sense of humiliation and hurt. Tears clouded her view and she began to cry, quietly at first, and then her sobs got louder. Intense rage overtook her and her sobbing became screams that pierced the quiet countryside. After a while, her crying subsided and she felt a sharp pain in her hand. She looked down and realized she still clenched tightly the neck of the broken Pepsi-Cola bottle. The jagged edges of glass had penetrated in between her thumb and forefinger; she was still bleeding. Releasing her grip, the young woman found a handkerchief in her pocket. Carefully she pressed it to the wound and in moments the bleeding stopped. Exhausted, she closed her eyes, leaned against the tree, and fell asleep.

She dreamt of that cool lakeside and the motorboat on the billboard that might take her back home to safety and comfort. Friends would be there, waiting, protection hers just for the asking.

"Wake up . . . it's all right. It's me, Ann." She felt a hand on her shoulder and opened her eyes. Ann was there, her eyes filled with kindness and concern. Again, the young woman cried, openly and without shame, as she embraced her friend.

"I know, we got your wire, but only after we got home. By then it was late, around three o'clock, and we went looking for you right away. This is a very small town. You caused quite a stir. I should have warned you about things out here. But, I thought it would be best to tell you when we were together. I'm so sorry . . . but don't worry . . . you are safe and with us. We are proud of you . . . the way you stood up . . . but, never mind that now. Let's get you home where you can rest. But, you were wonderful . . ."

In the weeks that followed, the young woman worked with Ann. She made lifetime friends in the small Texas community. There were others like her and like Ann, who would fight against those signs. Civil rights had to be won and the battles still had to be fought. She understood quite clearly in that summer of 1956, that no matter where she might settle, or in which direction life would take her, the work she would commit herself to, and indeed her existence itself, would be dedicated to the struggle and the fight against oppression. Consciously for the first time in her life, the young woman was proud of all she was, her skin, her hair and the fact that she was a woman.

Riding back East on the bus, she looked at her hand and realized the wound she had suffered had healed. However, two tiny scars remained, quite visible.

"A reminder . . . should I ever forget," she whispered softly.

Settling back, she let the rhythmic motion of the large bus lull her into a sweet sleep. The future with all its uncertainties was before her; now she was more than ready for this challenge.

AFTER YOU READ

Exchanging Backgrounds and Cultures

1. What does the wording of the sign in the cafe reveal about the owner's attitude toward African and Mexican Americans?

2. The young woman stands up to the owner and fights for her rights. What does this suggest about the kind of person she is?

3. Why does the young woman suddenly—and consciously—feel proud for the first time in her life? What does this tell you about her?

What Do You Think?

Which part of this selection has the greatest impact on you? What makes it so powerful?

Experiencing Fiction

In this short story, Mohr tells about a young woman's experience—an experience that gives her a new feeling of pride in herself as a Latina and a new sense of purpose. Think about an experience in your own life or in someone else's life that brought about a new sense of purpose. Write a short story that uses a narrator to tell about the experience and the understanding gained from it.

Optional Activity At the end of the story, the young woman feels proud of all that she is. What are you proud of about yourself? Write a short story that involves this sense of pride. Tell about what happened to make you feel proud. Write your story in the third person.

INTRODUCTION
Raining Backwards

Roberto G. Fernández (roh-BEHR-toh fer-NAHN-des) was born in Sagua la Grande, Cuba, and has lived in the United States since 1961. He belongs to a generation of Cuban writers who grew up and were educated in the United States. Fernández currently lives in Tallahassee, Florida, where he teaches Hispanic literature at Florida State University.

Fernández's third novel, *Raining Backwards*, received great praise from critics. The work was one of the first Cuban American novels to be written in English and published in the United States. One of the ways Fernández makes the characters in this novel seem true-to-life is through his use of dialogue containing nonstandard English. The story's dialogue reflects his cultural background. It also reveals Fernández's sensitivity to the way that people acquiring English may speak in everyday conversation. In the following excerpt from *Raining Backwards*, the narrator recalls his efforts to help his grandmother return to Cuba before she dies.

Raining Backwards

by Roberto G. Fernández

 "Michael, Miqui, Miguel. Come here!"

"Yes, abuela."[1]

"Your abuela is no waiting for the paramedics, no waiting for the ambulance. You hear that siren? The next one is for me, but they won't catch me!"

"Slowly, abuela. Slowly. Come again."

"I need your help. You help your abuela, okay? You love your abuela, right?"

"Okay, okay, Abuela, make it quick."

"The rescue, Miqui, the rescue, the paramedics, Miqui. Once they get you, they plug you in and you just cannot die. Besides, I no want to be bury in this country. I will be the first one here and who knows where the next one will be, dead and all alone! The whole world gets scatter in America, even dead people. When I am gone I want to be right next to my sister, Hilda, in Havana. I owe it to her. Me bury in Havana, okay? No here."

"Abuela, don't call me Miqui. You know I don't like it. What's your problem?"

---

1. **abuela** (ah-BWEH-lah) *n.* grandmother

"I am dying."

"C'mon. You aren't dying."

"Anytime now. I already have . . . let me think how many years I have. Mari, Mari, Mari-Clara,[2] child, you remember how many years I have?"

"Please mother! I'm trying to concentrate on this last posture. Don't bother me now."

"I know I have many. Anytime now. It was raining backwards yesterday. When my father died it was raining backwards also."

"There you go again, Abuela. It can't rain backwards! What a silly idea."

"Why you can no believe me? You think your abuela would trick you?"

"You had too much coffee, Abuela. Coffee makes you high. *Mucho cafe!*"[3]

"Why you can no believe me? I believe you when you told me many years ago that a man went to sleep for twenty years and when he woke up his beard reach his feet. I remember, I told it to Barbarita and Mirta. They were very impressed. I even told it to that woman that use to rent her daughter dressed as a flag for parties and political rallies. What was her name? You remember, Miqui?"

"Abuela, please. My name is Michael."

"Mari, Mari, Mari-Clara, you remember the name of that woman that use to rent her daughter for social events dressed as a flag?"

"Mother, please, you made me lose my concentration!"

"Anyway, abuela is no staying here, okay? Hilda is too

---

2. **Mari, Mari, Mari-Clara** (MAH-ree KLAH-rah) an exclamation; a mild oath
3. *Mucho cafe!* (MOO-choh kah-FEH) Lots of coffee!

alone without me and she needs me so much. I go accompany her!"

"But Hilda is dead. You told me so. Hilda is dead, Grandma!"

"Dead people feel alone too, they have feelings, you know. So you are going to help me, yes or no?"

"Okay, okay. What do you want me to do? But make it quick. I gotta be at the try-outs in half an hour. It's football season, Abuela."

"Mother, you're eighty-three. Her name was Emelina and her daughter's Linda Lucia."

The following morning, Abuela gave me the details of her flight, and I had to swear never to reveal her plan. After the swearing ceremony was over, I lent her a hand and we were on our way to the woods a few miles from the house. We went looking for a sturdy tree. In the midst of the thicket Abuela sniffed at a tall mahogany and said, "What you waiting for?" She placed a sharp ax in my hands and like a mad cheerleader started shouting, "Miqui, Miqui, cut it, cut it, rah-rah-rah." It was then that my eye caught a black seagull's nest perched on the mahogany's canopy. I knew that it was the sturdiest tree, but the black seagulls were on my Boy Scouts list of endangered species. I thought for a few minutes and told her that the mahogany was a sick tree. "You choose, now," said Abuela. I looked around, selecting an old perforated[4] oak. She smiled when I was able to bring it down with just a few blows.

"You cut good, Miqui. I like that!"

From then on, I followed her orders like a robot. She was so determined that I couldn't question her. She

---

4. **perforated** (PER-fuh-rayt-ihd) *adj.* full of holes

instructed me to start carving a hole right in the center of the tree.

"Come on. Take the arms off! Get the arms off the tree first!"

I didn't quite understand what she meant, and Abuela, losing her patience, grabbed the ax, dismembering[5] the unsuspecting vegetable. That afternoon the oak had the appearance of an old board being consumed by human termites. Then Abuela fell asleep for a couple of hours, while I continued laboring. She awoke, inspected the work and patted me on my back. I grinned while thinking that I had surely saved the black seagulls from an impetuous[6] old lady who I didn't quite understand.

For the next two months, we returned faithfully to our secret enterprise, where, camouflaged under a heavy cover of pine straw, the ark was being built. It had two compartments, one for sitting up and one to keep the canned goods and water pail. It had no self-propulsion,[7] but a fake wheel and a hole in which to place a white flag. She had patiently covered the exterior with rhinestones and pictures of Julio Iglesias[8] and German Garcia all pasted to the surface with Superglue.

One afternoon, the admiral, while inspecting the day's work, asked me a few questions to determine my nautical[9] knowledge. Somewhat ashamed, I told her that I could

---

5. **dismembering** (dihs-MEHM-buhr-ihng) *v.* cutting up
6. **impetuous** (ihm-PECH-oo-wuhs) *adj.* rushing into action with little thought
7. **self-propulsion** (SEHLF-proh-PUHL-shuhn) *n.* the act of moving forward on one's own
8. **Julio Iglesias** (HOO-lee-oh ee-GLEH-see-uhs) a contemporary popular Latino singer
9. **nautical** (NAWT-ih-kuhl) *adj.* of or having to do with ships, sailors, or the sea

doggie paddle. Very calmly, Abuela ordered me to go to the library and to obtain, using any means at my disposal, a navigational chart.

"Miqui, when you learn the chart, we are going to go to steal the pick-up truck of your father and put the canoe in the bed, then we go to the Key Biscayne Marina and we rent motor boat, understand you?"

"I guess so . . . "

"Then we go to tow the vessel to where the Gulf Stream flows. You know the Gulf Stream is very, very close. I heard it in a radio program. Then I go from the motor boat to the canoe and you cut the rope, understand you?"

"But why?"

"I am going South. I'm going away, Miqui, and I come back no more, no more."

"But you'll die on the way!"

"No worry. I will be there in two days. I get off the boat. I wave my white flag. I drink a cup of coffee. I take a taxi and head for where Hilda rests and then it will begin to rain backwards . . . "

So there I was in the library stealing a navigational chart from an old dilapidated[10] National Geographic. I remember I put it inside my underwear to avoid detection by the electronic sensor. When I got home, I opened it. Puzzled by its contents, I stored it in my bottom drawer. Learning that chart would take me almost three weeks. When I told her I had everything down pat, she went to her room, changed to her Sunday best and headed to catch a bus for Dadeland Mall with Mom's Gold American Express. When Abuela returned, she had bought two evening gowns, a flowery parasol[11] and seven tape players, which would have been the envy of any kid. She showed

---

10. **dilapidated** (dih-LAP-ih-DAYT-ihd) *adj.* run down due to neglect
11. **parasol** (PAR-uh-sawl) *n.* a small, light umbrella carried to protect someone from the sun

me her purchases, while repeating several times that she just couldn't arrive empty handed.

"The purple dress is for Hilda. Is low cut . . . ."

The big day came and Abuela was wearing a red sequined dress and carrying her parasol like an authentic tropical toreador.[12] I led her to the pick-up and, with great reverence, a la Walter Raleigh,[13] took her by the hand while opening the door. I was euphoric! For the first time in my life I was driving my father's truck. He was completely unaware of what we were doing, because he was partying with Mom. During the night, Abuela had managed to steal the keys from my father's drawer.

After a couple of jerky starts, we drove towards the woods. We got out of the truck and, after struggling for a while, with the help of three pulleys, we managed to place the canoe inside. It was around three in the morning. I was going to have my first solo drive along U.S. 1. I was so happy and Abuela was beaming. I pulled into the parking lot like a pro and went straight to the office. We rented the motor boat using Mom's credit card. . . .

We headed southeast in search of the Gulf Stream. Our boat was moving slowly. It wasn't easy to tow the refurbished[14] tree trunk. Abuela was really bubbly, talking incessantly,[15] telling me of everything from the day she caught her finger grinding coffee beans to the first kiss my grandfather gave her through the iron gates that covered the living room window. We were getting closer to the

---

12. **toreador** (TOHR-ee-uh-dohr) *n.* bullfighter
13. **Walter Raleigh** (WAWL-tuhr RAW-lee) Sir Walter Raleigh (c. 1552–1618), an English courtier, navigator, and historian who was known for his courtesy
14. **refurbished** (rih-FUHR-bihsht) *adj.* renovated; made like new
15. **incessantly** (ihn-SEHS-uhnt-lee) *adv.* in a way that seems endless

point where I thought the current would take her directly to her destination. The waters were turning deep blue. I slowed down, and Abuela, sensing that we were closing on the Gulf Stream, turned very thoughtful and, losing her previous effervescence,[16] said, "You know why I have to accompany Hilda? Well, I am going to tell you. The kiss your grandfather gave me was no for me, I knew that that afternoon he was going to pass by to see her because he had been enamoring her for almost a year, and then I covered my face with a silk veil and he kissed me through it, thoughting I was Hilda. Then I took the cover off my face and he was bewitched by me. Hilda died a lonely old maid throwing up stars."

"Stars?" I said.

"Yes, stars. It was God's way to reward her sufferings on earth. No believe me?"

"You can't throw up stars!"

"What if I tell you that she ate a can of chicken and stars soup before she died, you believe me now?"

"Well, it makes more sense . . . not a whole lot, but it makes more sense since she had the soup."

Abuela was in a trance for a few minutes, rewinding her mind. Then her voice was trembling when she added, "I have something more to tell you. It is no all. I cheated on your grandfather once in my life. Kirby was in love with me!"

"Kirby, the black bean soup maker?"

"No, Michael. No be ignorant. They teach you nothing in school? The poet. He was learning Spanish to talk to me because at that time I knew very little English. I remember he used to tell me in the factory, whispering in my ear, 'My poems are palest green and flaming scarlet, a wounded deer that searches for a refuge in the forest.'

---

16. effervescence (ehf-er-VEHS-ens) *n.* high spirits; enthusiasm

Pretty, eh? I memorized the lines, but I left him because he loved to say bad words and I no like ordinary people. We both worked for the Libby factory, it still makes peaches in heavy syrup. He was the foreman, but he disillusioned me because every day at five o'clock when the whistle sound he used to tell me, 'Nelia, *cojon*,[17] no more work, enough for today, *cojon*.' That is why I left him and we never became nothing. I never like ordinary people that say bad words."

"Abuela, he probably was saying 'go home' not 'cojon.'"

"Well, it is too late now. But I think I loved your grandfather the most."

After our last dialogue, Abuela stepped across a plank from the tow boat to the canoe as I was pulling the rope free from the tow. Her vessel was moving now in all directions. She smiled, threw me a kiss, and said, "You be good, Miqui, okay? Make sure your mother drinks her warm milk, your father has the paper at breakfast and your brothers' tennis shoes are always clean, and you no worry for me. If I have problems I buy them with the tape players. That is why I carry them with me. You be good Miqui, okay?"

I didn't look back. I started the motor and kept my eyes fixed on the horizon, heading for port.

The tides have come and gone thousands of times, and I have come to the same marina as many times just to gaze South. . . . A week ago, for the first time, I noticed that my shoes were soaked and my head was dry. It was raining backwards! Then I realized that rabbits can't lay eggs and that my time was coming. I told my grandson and

---

17. *cojón* (koh-HOHN) *interj.* an exclamation or curse expressing anger or frustration

he said, "Grandpa Mike, you had too much coffee." I went straight to the old chest and found the yellowish chart we had used. I studied it for a while. I was determined to land where she had. Suddenly I realized the arrows indicating the direction of the current were pointing northeast, not south, like I had thought. I had read it upside down, or maybe backwards. I pictured Abuela's frozen figure in her sequined dress, holding her parasol inside some floating iceberg off the coast of Norway, having died alone like an old tropical Viking. Somehow I felt the iceberg's chill. Then the ambulance's siren brought me back from what I thought was simply a deep slumber and someone was shouting, "Mouth to mouth! Give him mouth to mouth. Get some air in his lungs. Hook him up to the machine!"

AFTER YOU READ

Exchanging Backgrounds and Cultures

1. What are Abuela's reasons for wanting to be buried in Cuba rather than in the United States?

2. Do you think Abuela's feelings are common to other people who have immigrated to the United States? Explain your answer.

3. What does this selection reveal about Abuela's personality?

What Do You Think?

Which part of this story is most surprising to you? What makes it so surprising?

Experiencing Fiction

Writers often choose to tell a story from a first-person point of view. The character uses the word *I* instead of *he* or *she*. In this selection, Miguel tells the story from the first-person point of view. Why do you think the author does this?

Think about the events of this past year. Does anything stand out in your mind? Write a short story to tell about that experience. Use the first-person point of view and include dialogue, as Fernández does.

Optional Activity At the end of this episode, the narrator—now a dying, elderly man—realizes the tragic error he made so many years ago. Write a fictional episode about an error someone makes. This could be a humorous episode about an error in something said or done. It could be about a tragic error, like the one Fernández describes. Try using the first-person narrative.

INTRODUCTION
American History

Julia Ortiz Cofer (HOOL-yah ohr-TEES KOH-fer) is both a poet and a novelist. Born in Hormigueros, Puerto Rico, she moved to Paterson, New Jersey, when her father was transferred there with the U.S. Army. Where she lived and attended school depended on where her military father was sent. She lived for long periods of time in Puerto Rico, which enabled her to expose the cultures of both Puerto Rico and the United States in her writing.

Cofer graduated from Augusta College in Georgia, the state in which she now lives, received a master's degree from Florida Atlantic University, and attended Oxford University in England. She has received many awards for her writing.

For the short story you are about to read, "American History," Cofer chose a familiar setting—the multiethnic neighborhood in her former hometown of Paterson. The story revolves around the reactions of people to the assassination of President John F. Kennedy on November 22, 1963. At the same time, it centers on a Puerto Rican teenager's thoughts, feelings, and actions on that very day.

American History

by Judith Ortiz Cofer

I once read in a "Ripley's Believe It or Not" column that Paterson, New Jersey, is the place where the Straight and Narrow (streets) intersect. The Puerto Rican tenement known as *El Building* was one block up from Straight. It was, in fact, the corner of Straight and Market; not "at" the corner, but *the* corner. At almost any hour of the day, El Building was like a monstrous jukebox, blasting out *salsas*[1] from open windows as the residents, mostly new immigrants just up from the island, tried to drown out whatever they were currently enduring with loud music. But the day President Kennedy was shot there was a profound silence in El Building; even the abusive tongues of viragoes,[2] the cursing of the unemployed, and the screeching of small children had been somehow muted. President Kennedy was a saint to these people. In fact, soon his photograph would be hung alongside the Sacred Heart and over the spiritist altars that many women kept in their apartments. He would become part of the hierarchy of martyrs they prayed to for favors that only one who had died for a cause would understand.

---

1. *salsas* (SAHL-sahs) *n. pl.* a kind of music (literally, *sauces*)
2. **viragoes** (vuh-RAHG-ohz) *n. pl.* loud, overbearing women

On the day that President Kennedy was shot, my ninth grade class had been out in the fenced playground of Public School Number 13. We had been given "free" exercise time and had been ordered by our P.E. teacher, Mr. DePalma, to "keep moving." That meant that the girls should jump rope and the boys toss basketballs through a hoop at the far end of the yard. He in the meantime would "keep an eye" on us from just inside the building.

It was a cold gray day in Paterson. The kind that warns of early snow. I was miserable, since I had forgotten my gloves, and my knuckles were turning red and raw from the jump rope. I was also taking a lot of abuse from the black girls for not turning the rope hard and fast enough for them.

"Hey, Skinny Bones, pump it, girl. Ain't you got no energy today?" Gail, the biggest of the black girls had the other end of the rope, yelled, "Didn't you eat your rice and beans and pork chops for breakfast today?"

The other girls picked up the "pork chop" and made it into a refrain: "pork chop, pork chop, did you eat your pork chop?" They entered the double ropes in pairs and exited without tripping or missing a beat. I felt a burning on my cheeks and then my glasses fogged up so that I could not manage to coordinate the jump rope with Gail. The chill was doing to me what it always did; entering my bones, making me cry, humiliating me. I hated the city, especially in winter. I hated Public School Number 13. I hated my skinny flatchested body, and I envied the black girls who could jump rope so fast that their legs became a blur. They always seemed to be warm while I froze.

There was only one source of beauty and light for me that school year. The only thing I had anticipated at the start of the semester. That was seeing Eugene. In August, Eugene and his family had moved into the only house on the block that had a yard and trees. I could see his place from my window in El Building. In fact, if I sat on the fire escape I was literally suspended above Eugene's backyard. It was my favorite spot to read my library books in the summer. Until that August the house had been occupied by an old Jewish couple. Over the years I had become part of their family, without their knowing it, of course. I had a view of their kitchen and their backyard, and though I could not hear what they said, I knew when they were arguing, when one of them was sick, and many other things. I knew all this by watching them at mealtimes. I could see their kitchen table, the sink, and the stove. During good times, he sat at the table and read his newspapers while she fixed the meals. If they argued, he would leave and the old woman would sit and stare at nothing for a long time. When one of them was sick, the other would come and get things from the kitchen and carry them out on a tray. The old man had died in June. The last week of school I had not seen him at the table at all. Then one day I saw that there was a crowd in the kitchen. The old woman had finally emerged from the house on the arm of a stocky, middle-aged woman, whom I had seen there a few times before, maybe her daughter. Then a man had carried out suitcases. The house had stood empty for weeks. I had had to resist the temptation to climb down into the yard and water the flowers the old lady had taken such good care of.

By the time Eugene's family moved in, the yard was a tangled mass of weeds. The father had spent several days mowing, and when he finished, from where I sat, I didn't see the red, yellow, and purple clusters that meant flowers to me. I didn't see this family sit down at the kitchen table together. It was just the mother, a red-headed tall woman who wore a white uniform—a nurse's, I guessed it was; the father was gone before I got up in the morning and was never there at dinner time. I only saw him on weekends when they sometimes sat on lawn-chairs under the oak tree, each hidden behind a section of the newspaper; and there was Eugene. He was tall and blond, and he wore glasses. I liked him right away because he sat at the kitchen table and read books for hours. That summer, before we had even spoken one word to each other, I kept him company on my fire escape.

Once school started I looked for him in all my classes, but P.S. 13 was a huge, over-populated place and it took me days and many discreet questions to discover that Eugene was in honors classes for all his subjects; classes that were not open to me because English was not my first language, though I was a straight A student. After much maneuvering I managed "to run into him" in the hallway where his locker was—on the other side of the building from mine— and in study hall at the library where he first seemed to notice me, but did not speak; and finally, on the way home after school one day when I decided to approach him directly, though my stomach was doing somersaults.

I was ready for rejection, snobbery, the worst. But when I came up to him, practically panting in my nervousness, and blurted out: "You're Eugene. Right?" he smiled, pushed his glasses up on his nose, and nodded. I saw then that he was blushing deeply. Eugene liked me, but he was shy. I did most of the talking that day. He nodded and smiled a lot. In the weeks that followed, we walked home together. He would linger at the corner of El Building for a few minutes then walk down to his two-story house. It was not until Eugene moved into that house that I noticed that El Building blocked most of the sun, and that the only spot that got a little sunlight during the day was the tiny square of earth the old woman had planted with flowers.

I did not tell Eugene that I could see inside his kitchen from my bedroom. I felt dishonest, but I liked my secret sharing of his evenings, especially now that I knew what he was reading since we chose our books together at the school library.

One day my mother came into my room as I was sitting on the window sill staring out. In her abrupt way she said: "Elena, you are acting 'moony.'" *Enamorada*[3] was what she really said, that is—like a girl stupidly infatuated. . . . My mother was unhappy in Paterson, but my father had a good job at the bluejeans factory in Passaic and soon, he kept assuring us, we would be moving to our own house there. Every Sunday we drove out to the suburbs of Paterson, Clifton, and Passaic, out to where people mowed grass on Sundays in the summer, and where children made snowmen in the winter from pure white snow, not like the gray slush of Paterson which seemed to fall from the sky in that hue. I had learned to listen to my parents' dreams, which were spoken in Spanish, as fairy tales, like the stories about life in the island paradise of Puerto Rico before I was born. I had been to the island once as a little girl, to grandmother's funeral, and all I remembered was wailing women in black, my mother becoming hysterical and being given a pill that made her sleep two days, and me feeling lost in a crowd of strangers all claiming to be my aunts, uncles, and cousins. I had actually been glad to return to the city. We had not been back there since then, though my parents talked constantly about buying a house on the beach someday, retiring on the island—that was a common topic among the residents of El Building. As for me, I was going to go to college and become a teacher.

But after meeting Eugene I began to think of the present more than of the future. What I wanted now was to enter that house I had watched for so many years. I wanted to see the other rooms where the old people had lived, and where the boy spent his time. Most of all, I

---

3. *Enamorada* (eh-nahm-uh-RAHD-ah) *adj.* charmed; captivated

wanted to sit at the kitchen table with Eugene like two adults, like the old man and his wife had done, maybe drink some coffee and talk about books. I had started reading *Gone With the Wind*. I was enthralled[4] by it, with the daring and the passion of the beautiful girl living in a mansion, and with her devoted parents and the slaves who did everything for them. I didn't believe such a world had ever really existed, and I wanted to ask Eugene some questions since he and his parents, he had told me, had come up from Georgia, the same place where the novel was set. His father worked for a company that had transferred him to Paterson. His mother was very unhappy, Eugene said, in his beautiful voice that rose and fell over words in a strange, lilting way. The kids at school called him "the hick" and made fun of the way he talked. I knew I was his only friend so far, and I liked that, though I felt sad for him sometimes. "Skinny Bones" and the "Hick" was what they called us at school when we were seen together.

The day Mr. DePalma came out into the cold and asked us to line up in front of him was the day that President Kennedy was shot. Mr. DePalma, a short, muscular man with slicked-down black hair, was the science teacher, P.E. coach, and disciplinarian at P.S. 13. He was the teacher to whose homeroom you got assigned if you were a troublemaker, and the man called out to break up playground fights, and to escort violently angry teen-agers to the office. And Mr. DePalma was the man who called your parents in for "a conference."

That day, he stood in front of two rows of mostly black and Puerto Rican kids, brittle from their efforts to "keep moving" on a November day that was turning bitter cold.

---

4. **enthralled** (ihn-THRAWLD) *adj.* charmed; fascinated

Mr. DePalma, to our complete shock, was crying. Not just silent adult tears, but really sobbing. There were a few titters from the back of the line where I stood shivering.

"Listen," Mr. DePalma raised his arms over his head as if he were about to conduct an orchestra. His voice broke, and he covered his face with his hands. His barrel chest was heaving. Someone giggled behind me.

"Listen," he repeated, "something awful has happened." A strange gurgling came from his throat, and he turned around and spat on the cement behind him.

"Gross," someone said, and there was a lot of laughter.

"The President is dead, you idiots. I should have known that wouldn't mean anything to a bunch of losers like you kids. Go home." He was shrieking now. No one moved for a minute or two, but then a big girl let out a "Yeah!" and ran to get her books piled up with the others against the brick wall of the school building. The others followed in a mad scramble to get to their things before somebody caught on. It was still an hour to the dismissal bell.

A little scared, I headed for El Building. There was an eerie feeling on the streets. I looked into Mario's drugstore, a favorite hangout for the high school crowd, but there were only a couple of old Jewish men at the soda-bar talking with the short order cook in tones that sounded almost angry, but they were keeping their voices low. Even the traffic on one of the busiest intersections in Paterson—Straight Street and Park Avenue—seemed to be moving slower. There were no horns blasting that day. At El Building, the usual little group of unemployed men were not hanging out on the front stoop making it difficult for women to enter the front door. No music spilled out from open doors in the hallway. When I walked into our apartment, I found my mother sitting in front of the grainy picture of the television set.

She looked up at me with a tear-streaked face and just said: "Dios mio,"[5] turning back to the set as if it were pulling at her eyes. I went into my room.

Though I wanted to feel the right thing about President Kennedy's death, I could not fight the feeling of elation that stirred my chest. Today was the day I was to visit Eugene in his house. He had asked me to come over after school to study for an American History test with him. We had also planned to walk to the public library together. I looked down into his yard. The oak tree was bare of leaves and the ground looked gray with ice. The light through the large kitchen window of his house told me that El Building blocked the sun to such an extent that they had to run lights on in the middle of the day. I felt ashamed about it. But the white kitchen table with the lamp hanging just above it looked cozy and inviting. I would soon sit there, across from Eugene, and I would tell him about my perch just above his house. Maybe I should.

In the next thirty minutes I changed clothes, put on a little pink lipstick, and got my books together. Then I went in to tell my mother that I was going to a friend's house to study. I did not expect her reaction.

"You are going out *today*?" The way she said "today" sounded as if a storm warning had been issued. It was said in utter disbelief. Before I could answer, she came toward me and held my elbows as I clutched my books.

"*Hija*,[6] the President has been killed. We must show respect. He was a great man. Come to church with me tonight."

She tried to embrace me, but my books were in the

---

5. **Dios mio** (dyohs MEE-oh) My God
6. *Hija* (EE-hah) *n.* daughter

way. My first impulse was to comfort her, she seemed so distraught, but I had to meet Eugene in fifteen minutes.

"I have a test to study for, Mama. I will be home by eight."

"You are forgetting who you are, *Niña*.[7] I have seen you staring down at that boy's house. You are heading for humiliation and pain." My mother said this in Spanish and in a resigned tone that surprised me, as if she had no intention of stopping me from "heading for humiliation and pain." I started for the door. She sat in front of the TV holding a white handkerchief to her face.

I walked out to the street and around the chain-link fence that separated El Building from Eugene's house. The yard was neatly edged around the little walk that led to the door. It always amazed me how Paterson, the inner core of the city, had no apparent logic to its architecture. Small, neat, single residences like this one could be found right next to huge, dilapidated apartment buildings like El Building. My guess was that the little houses had been there first, then immigrants had come in droves, and the monstrosities had been raised for them—the Italians, the Irish, the Jews, and now us, the Puerto Ricans and the blacks. The door was painted a deep green: *verde*, the color of hope, I had heard my mother say it: *Verde-Esperanza*.[8]

I knocked softly. A few suspenseful moments later the door opened just a crack. The red, swollen face of a woman appeared. She had a halo of red hair floating over a delicate ivory face—the face of a doll—with freckles on the nose. Her smudged eye make-up made her look unreal to me, like a mannequin seen through a warped store window.

---

7. *Niña* (NEEN-yah) *n.* girl
8. *Verde-Esperanza* (VEHR-deh-ehs-peh-RAHN-sah) green-hope

"What do you want?" Her voice was tiny and sweet-sounding, like a little girl's, but her tone was not friendly.

"I'm Eugene's friend. He asked me over. To study." I thrust out my books, a silly gesture that embarrassed me almost immediately.

"You live there?" She pointed up to El Building, which looked particularly ugly, like a gray prison with its many dirty windows and rusty fire escapes. The woman had stepped halfway out and I could see that she wore a white nurse's uniform with St. Joseph's Hospital on the name tag.

"Yes. I do."

She looked intently at me for a couple of heartbeats, then said as if to herself, "I don't know how you people do it." Then directly to me: "Listen. Honey. Eugene doesn't want to study with you. He is a smart boy. Doesn't need help. You understand me. I am truly sorry if he told you you could come over. He cannot study with you. It's nothing personal. You understand? We won't be in this place much longer, no need for him to get close to people—it'll just make it harder for him later. Run back home now."

I couldn't move. I just stood there in shock at hearing these things said to me in such a honey-drenched voice. I had never heard an accent like hers, except for Eugene's softer versions. It was as if she were singing me a little song.

"What's wrong? Didn't you hear what I said?" She seemed very angry, and I finally snapped out of my trance. I turned away from the green door, and heard her close it gently.

Our apartment was empty when I got home. My mother was in someone else's kitchen, seeking the solace she needed. Father would come in from his late shift at midnight. I would hear them talking softly in the kitchen for hours that night. They would not discuss their dreams for the future, or life in Puerto Rico, as they often did; that night they would talk sadly about the young widow and her two children, as if they were family. For the next few days, we would observe *luto*[9] in our apartment; that is, we would practice restraint and silence—no loud music or laughter. Some of the women of El Building would wear black for weeks.

That night, I lay in my bed trying to feel the right thing for our dead President. But the tears that came up from a deep source inside me were strictly for me. When my mother came to the door, I pretended to be sleeping. Sometime during the night, I saw from my bed the streetlight come on. It had a pink halo around it. I went to my window and pressed my face to the cool glass. Looking up at the light I could see the white snow falling like a lace veil over its face. I did not look down to see it turning gray as it touched the ground below.

---

9. *luto* (LOO-toh) *n.* mourning; sorrow; bereavement

AFTER YOU READ

Exchanging Backgrounds and Cultures

1. The main character wants to stay in the United States, while her parents talk about returning to Puerto Rico. What do the family members' differences tell you about them as individuals?

2. When Mr. DePalma announces President Kennedy's death, he is upset and angry. Why do you think he takes out his anger on the students?

3. Does this story reflect only the experiences of a Puerto Rican teenager, or could this happen to a teenager of any background? Explain your thoughts.

What Do You Think?

Which part of the story is especially meaningful to you? Why is it so important?

Experiencing Fiction

Through the fictional character of Elena, Judith Ortiz Cofer explores her own experiences of growing up. Write a short story based on an experience in your own life by creating a fictional character who has that same experience. Use a setting that is familiar to you. Include descriptions and dialogue to show the character's thoughts and feelings, actions and reactions.

Optional Activity In "American History," Elena is rejected by her friend's mother. Write a story about a character who is rejected by someone. How does this character react to the rejection? Remember to develop the character through his or her own thoughts, feelings, dialogue, and actions.

INTRODUCTION
Latin Jazz

Virgil Suarez (veer-HEEL swah-RES) was born in Havana, Cuba, in 1962 and lived there until 1970, when his family moved to Madrid, Spain. In 1974, the family moved to the United States and settled in Los Angeles. Suarez received degrees from California State University and Louisiana State University. He currently teaches at Louisiana State University in Baton Rouge, where he also lives and writes. Suarez is the author of many short stories that have appeared in literary and university magazines. He has also written numerous articles, reviews, interviews, and two novels.

The selection you are about to read is taken from *Latin Jazz*, Suarez's novel based on his experiences as a Latino living in Los Angeles. In this novel, Suarez draws upon his own background to tell about the experiences of a family that leaves Cuba after Fidel Castro comes to power. Suarez describes the problems the family faces after settling in the United States. He also tells about a member of this family who is caught up in the Cuban Revolution.

from *Latin Jazz*

by Virgil Suarez

ANGEL/Los Angeles, city of skyscrapers under ashen skies where so many windows give the impression of individual wasp hives that reflect smoggy skies and more across-the-way hives. Too many cars, buses, trucks. City of speed and races.

For Angel Falcón, Los Angeles brings back memories of when the family had first arrived from Cuba in 1962. They lived on Pico in a three-story apartment building not too far from where they are now passing. He and his wife, Lilián, drive through the downtown panic of pedestrians trying to cross streets, even when the street signals flash: DON'T WALK!

Strewn newspapers and crushed cans clutter the streets and sidewalks, gather by the curb and gutters. Spoiled fruit rots in broken crates. . . .

People witness two bums fighting over a wine bottle under a fire escape in an alley. Three times a week Angel and his wife come downtown to buy merchandise wholesale to sell in the ice cream truck. Nothing has changed. The poorly dressed Mexican children with hungry looks on their faces remind him of the harshness and struggle of the first days in California, the constant trips to the immigration department.

When he sells the merchandise through the streets of Bell and South Gate—suburbs of the big city—he can see the despair. What a name for a city so full of sin and evil and chaos. The Angels.

The years have gone by quickly, and Angel sees himself, the family, moving farther and farther away from Los Angeles. They can now afford to, he thinks. Lilián and he do their business in Bell, but they live on Evergreen Street, a residential block in South Gate.

It is a humble, three-bedroom, two-bathroom house—Diego, their son, sleeps in the den. Angel likes the back room best because the breeze keeps it cool during the summer afternoons, for whatever little time he isn't out selling.

Angel and Lilián have never been this much together, but now they share at least nine to ten hours a day riding around, selling ice cream, making a decent living. They bought the ice cream truck with the money they managed to save by working at odd jobs, factory work mostly. Perhaps it's what Diego accuses them of that is true: They avoid the problems at home by hiding within the comfortable numbness, motor-warmth of the truck. When they're through for the day, they go home, shower, eat and go to sleep to rest up for the next day.

Seven years ago they started the ice cream business, six months after Concha, Angel's mother-in-law, died. Concha, who always had stories about the past up her sleeve. She often spoke of the good times . . .

He works seven days a week, including holidays when Lilián may stay home and do the household chores. American holidays are the best-selling days. What more can he ask for, considering that the day they crossed the ninety miles from Varadero[1] to Key West, they had nothing but three ragged suitcases filled with old clothes.

---

1. **Varadero** (vah-rah-DEH-roh) a city on the Peninsula de Hicacos in northwestern Cuba

Lilián, like her mother, likes to reminisce about how things used to be for the family, the "good days" as she likes to refer to them, before her brother Hugo left the university to join the rebels in Sierra Maestra. Angel, too, has lived through better, like when he owned the two cafeterias in Santiago, on José Martí Street, but why complain? Why bring back something that died the day he arrived in this country?

Esteban, his father-in-law, lives with them. The old man keeps himself busy by doing little odds and ends around the house, watering the flowers or raking dead leaves, but Esteban has never forgotten the past, for in the past he lost, as he says, his identity, dignity, his respect for humanity. In the past or inside the motherland, he still believes that Hugo's alive and well, though the last time they heard from him he was in Mazorra.[2]

Details are hard to keep track of, Angel knows, especially when they have to do with such a stubborn person as Hugo. The truth of the matter is that Angel and Hugo never got along because of Hugo's ideology. Back then he was an idealist, who believed the way to power and justice was through force. Lilián keeps her brother's letters and journal entries somewhere. Hugo could have come down from the hills when it was time to go, time for him to realize that the revolution was being fought for all the wrong reasons.

Because Hugo had not returned from the sierras,[3] Esteban and Concha didn't want to leave. A chain reaction occurred. Lilián wouldn't leave without her parents, so they waited and waited. Finally, after Hugo was arrested and sentenced to twenty years, the family left.

Angel never talks about past mistakes or whose fault it was they didn't leave Cuba sooner because Esteban doesn't

2. Mazorra (muh-ZAWR-ruh) a psychiatric hospital in Havana, Cuba
3. sierras (see-EH-rahs) *n. pl.* mountain ridges

like to be reminded of how much better things could have turned out.

Time flies, Angel thinks, at supersonic speeds. His days begin and end the same: with work.

They buy the merchandise from different places. Candies, toys, soft drinks, ice creams. Today he rushes from the candy and toy warehouse in Los Angeles to the ice cream factory near where he lives. It's a new place owned by compatriots, Bebo and Eloisa, a nice family. Julio Iglesias plays on a radio sitting on a shelf behind the cash register. Lilián usually goes to the back where there is a sofa and two armchairs on which to sit and chats with Bebo's wife about her golden years in Santiago before the revolution when she was part of the Highlife on Vista Alegre. . . .

CONCHA/Mama Concha's medley, medley of past lives without which present life would be unbearable. Three days before she died at Saint Francis of Assisi Hospital, she sent for her grandson Diego. Not that he was the only person she wanted to see, but there was a particular reason why he had to hear what she wanted to say.

The boy (this is what she called him, this and sometimes Diegito), she knew the boy was growing up rootless, or, as her own mother—her soul rest in glory—would have put it, wild . . . .

Before the stomach cancer, while she was still at home, she heard her daughter Lilián argue with him about forgetting the language, how little Spanish he spoke, his poor pronunciation. He showed no interest in his heritage or in knowing what had brought him here to this magnificent land.

He needed to relearn his background, Concha thought. This was the only way he could find identity and self-confidence. He had become too Americanized. Gringo.[4] Rootless. And she also knew that anybody who grew up rootless eventually lost his or her soul to . . .

The past was all important.

Diego came on a sunny afternoon, shortly after her siesta and bath. One of the nurses combed her hair and put a little rouge on her cheeks, but no lipstick. She never wore lipstick, didn't need to. Her lips possessed that deep crimson she had always been complimented for when she was a young lady.

Already aware of what the doctor had told him, that she wasn't going to last more than a couple of weeks (the cancer was diagnosed too late), he stood by the bed, a one-hundred-and-thirty-pound weakling, large, hungry-eyed, sweaty complexion, not a boy accustomed to smiling, tall and wiry in his slimness. At seventeen he was as tall as his Uncle Hugo before he ran up to the sierras and fought on the rebel side.

Hugo! What she wouldn't have given to have seen her son one last time.

She took a deep breath and gestured for her grandson to sit by her bed on the blue-cushioned chair. He, aloof so it seemed, dragged his feet as he walked over and sat next to the IV fork.

She wanted to know what the doctors had told him. Doctors, she knew, were capable of exaggerating, or making things sound a lot worse than they really were. She asked him to be nice to her because . . . she laughed at her melodramatic[5] thoughts.

---

4. **Gringo** (GREEN-goh) *n.* a foreigner in Spain or Latin America, especially of English or American origin
5. **melodramatic** (mehl-oh-druh-MAT-ihk) *adj.* emotional

"Don't think I'm sad," she said to him. "I am glad I've lived the life I have."

Diego sat shrouded in silence, his fingers gripping the chair's armrest.

"I want to tell you stories, son," she said. "Some, I'm sure, you've heard before, others you—you were never told."

"What kind of stories?" asked Diego.

"Good stories. About the family," she said.

"The doctor says you should rest."

"To hell with the doctor," she said and paused to gather her thoughts. "What I'm about to tell you might not make sense, but one day . . . promise to remind them . . . once in a while . . . especially your grandfather. Don't let him forget why we came to this country . . .

"*Curunguango guango, curunguango guango curungua tere me aguano curo . . .* ,[6] which, according to Marcelina, the woman who cooked for us in Vista Alegre, meant, Pay attention, pay attention, attend to the extraordinary thing I'm going to relate."

HUGO/The rain stops. I wake up to its silence. The sun has come out and dried my clothes which hang awkwardly from the window. Not completely, though. The pockets of my pants and the inseam feel damp. Should have turned them inside out, fool. The shirt too.

I dress and go downstairs. Once on the street, I start to retrace my steps to the post office to find a taxi. The sidewalks are wet and muddy. A stream of water carrying leaves and newspaper flows in the gutter.

---

6. *Curunguango guango, curunguango guango curungua tere me aguano curo* (koo-roon-GWAHN-goh GWAHN-goh koo-roon-GWAHN-goh GWAHN-goh koo-ROON-gwah TEHR-eh MEH ah-GWAHN-oh KOO-roh)

The shirt fits me more tightly now. Must have shrunk, but it doesn't look wrinkled. The pants do. Nothing can be done about that tear at the knee. Forget it.

The good thing about taxi drivers—at least this was true of them in Santiago—is that they never ask why you want to go where you tell them, but the one who picks me up does. He wants to know why Mazorra.

"My girlfriend works there," I tell him.

"Is it true that they're going to take the crazies to Mariel?"[7] the man says.

"Where did you hear that?" I say, leaning forward.

"Somebody told me. It's probably a rumor."

Lucinda's waiting, I'm sure she is. She knows I'm coming for her. I told her I would first chance I got.

The taxi driver turns on the radio to music, Tejedor and his orchestra. The man sings along. When I lean over to ask him where I can buy a sandwich or something else to eat because I'm starving, I see that his right arm's gone. His shirt sleeve is safety-pinned to his shirt.

"What are you staring at?" the man asks, looking at me from the corner of his eye.

"Nothing," I tell him. "Know where I can buy something to eat?"

"*Por aquí nada*,"[8] he says. "Everything's closed. This city's been wild since the break-in."

"Forget it then," I say.

The tune ends and the man turns the radio off. The ticks of the meter sound loud in the cab. "Got it blown off," he says. "I didn't even feel it."

"Where?" I ask.

---

7. **Mariel** (mahr-YEHL) a port about 30 miles from Havana, Cuba
8. *Por aquí nada* (pohr ah-KEE NAH-dah) Nothing here

"Angola,"[9] he says and looks up at the rearview mirror.
"That's too bad."

"Not really," he says, "in a way I'm glad it happened. I knew a lot of other guys who lost more than an arm."

"I know what you mean."

"What? You were there?"

"No." How old does he think I am? "In the revolution."

"Revolution?" He lets out a short laugh. "Are you serious?"

"I fought with comandante Morales. Lobo Morales."

"That was a long time ago," he says. Then, "So you're with the Party?"

The taxi driver senses my reluctance to talk so he looks up at the mirror and smiles. He's got a big scar under his right eye which makes that eye look smaller than the other.

"You know," he says, "after this happened, I had a chance to join the Party but didn't. And here I am now, driving this piece of shit."

"It gets you around, doesn't it?"

"Whenever it wants to. Parts are scarce."

"It seems to work all right," I say.

"What have you been doing all this time?"

"In jail."

"You kill somebody?" the man sounds excited to have somebody to converse with in the car.

"See, when Fidel[10] ordered Camilo Cienfuegos to

---

9. **Angola** (an-GOH-luh) a country in Africa; in 1975, Cuba intervened in a civil war for Angolan independence that led to a power struggle between Soviet-backed forces and Cubans against South African and Western-backed forces
10. **Fidel** (fee-DEHL) Fidel Castro, the president of Cuba

arrest Lobo Morales in Santiago, I was Lobo's aide. When the soldiers came for him, they took me too. Everybody in our unit was taken in. They even arrested this thirteen-year-old girl—"

"Wasn't Lobo the one who said that communism was infiltrating[11] the revolution?"

I say, "He was the smartest and bravest man I've ever known."

"He's dead?"

"A firing squad killed him."

They took Lucinda, so young, and I never saw her again until Mazorra.

We reach the corner of the dead-end street that leads to the front gate of Mazorra.

"Go to the embassy," I tell him. "You've got no future here."

"I'm afraid I can't do that," he says. "My wife doesn't want to leave. She waited for me while I was in Angola."

I understand his loyalty. "Drop me off before we get there," I say, reading the amount I owe him on the meter. Thirteen pesos.[12] I drop twenty on his lap. "Keep the change," I tell him.

The man pulls to the side and stops the car. He looks back and thanks me. "Maybe we'll run into each other," he says.

"Good luck," I say. I step out of the car and close the door behind me.

Soon it'll be dark and I can move in and try to find Lucinda. The man makes a U-turn and heads back to the main road. I watch him go until the car turns and vanishes around the bend, then I cross the street, jump the fence

---

11. **infiltrating** (ihn-fihl-TRAYT-ihng) *v.* entering or filtering into
12. **pesos** (PEH-sohs) *n. pl.* units of currency

upon which a NO TRESPASSING sign has been posted, and run around to the back of the building.

The new Havana zoo lies beyond the ravine.

The mangoes high up on the trees look ripe enough. I climb one of the trees slowly so as not to scrape the insides of my thighs on the thick bark. Once at the top, I knock a couple of mangoes down. Dinner.

In the ravine I find a place to remain out of sight, behind a tree stump. The grass surrounding me is really ivy.

Peeled, the mangoes are green and hard and taste sour. It'll be a while before they can be eaten. I eat a couple anyway.

The tall fence encircling Mazorra won't be a problem to jump over. Lucinda's window shouldn't be hard to spot. She's got all those plants on her sill. It's in the left wing of the building. Her window might be open, since she enjoys the cool breeze in the evening.

Judging from the darkness of the sky, I guess the time to be between five and six. One more hour and it'll be dark enough. Birds begin to nestle up in the trees for the night.

Still hungry, I contemplate knocking down some more mangoes. Something to do to kill time. If she only knew how close I am to her. A tiger roars and the sound strikes panic among the birds up in the trees. . . .

AFTER YOU READ

Exchanging Backgrounds and Cultures

1. In what ways are Angel and Hugo different? How do these differences affect their lives?
2. What does Concha's concern about Diego's "Americanization" reveal about her attitude toward the family's heritage?
3. Recall Hugo's conversation with the taxi driver and his plans to rescue Lucinda. What do his words and his behavior reveal about his attitude toward the Cuban government?

What Do You Think?

Which part of this selection makes the strongest impression on you? Why is this part of the story meaningful?

Experiencing Fiction

This selection presents the viewpoints of three different characters. Each section presents a different perspective from people who have lived through similar experiences. Think about a single experience that might have been viewed differently by different people. Write a short story that uses one narrator to describe the experience from the point of view of each of these people.

Optional Activity Concha wants to tell her grandson, Diego, about his heritage before she dies. Is there something in your heritage that you would want others to know about? Write a short story in which you share your memories and traditions with someone who may be unfamiliar with your culture.

UNIT 2: FOCUS ON WRITING

Young writers are often advised to write about what they know best. Although works of fiction spring from a writer's imagination, writers of short stories and novels usually draw upon their personal experiences and their cultural backgrounds. For example, in "American History" Judith Ortiz Cofer drew upon her childhood experiences in a multicultural neighborhood in Paterson, New Jersey.

Writing a Short Story

Short stories usually center on a single character, episode, conflict, or theme. Write a short story that tells about a personal conflict a character faces. This can be based on a personal experience or something you have made up.

The Writing Process

Good writing requires both time and effort. An effective writer completes a number of stages that together make up the writing process. The stages of the writing process are given below to help guide you through your assignment.

Prewriting

Begin by listing ideas that you think might make a good story. Then set up a chart with columns for these story elements: *setting, characters, conflict, plot, theme.* As you shape your story in your mind, make notes in each column. Questions like these will help you:

Setting: Where and when does the story take place? How will I describe this place and give a sense of this time?

Characters: Who is the main character? What other characters will take part in the action? How will I reveal the personality of each character? For example, in "Raining Backwards," we get to know Abuela through her grandson's eyes.

Conflict: What is the central problem? Is it internal (within the character's mind) or external (between the character and some outside force)?

Plot: What events will take place? What event will show the conflict? What will be the high point, or climax, of the story? How will the conflict be resolved?

Theme: Will the story have a message for the reader? If it does, how will the story reveal this message?

Before you begin writing, decide how you will tell the story. A narrator can be a character in the story as in "American History" and "Raining Backwards," or it can be someone who seems to be watching the events of the story as they happen, as in "An Awakening . . . Summer 1956" and "Latin Jazz."

Drafting and Revising

As you begin your draft of the story, refer to your prewriting chart. Your first draft is not the final version of the story, so write freely. You will be able to revise the draft later.

As you review your first draft, check to see that you have developed your characters through dialogue and action. Be sure you have included descriptions of sights, sounds, and even smells to give a sense of place. Make sure you have developed the plot in a way that will hold the reader's interest.

Proofreading and Publishing

After you have finished revising your short story, proofread it carefully. Correct any errors in spelling, grammar, punctuation, and capitalization. Then make a neat final copy.

Think about how you might share this story with others. You may want to read it aloud to your classmates, family, or friends. You may want to submit it to a school literary magazine or to a national magazine that publishes student writing.

UNIT 3

POETRY OF THE LATINO CARIBBEANS

There are as many definitions of poetry as there are poets. Poetry takes many forms, and poets use a wide variety of writing techniques and styles to express their thoughts.

Repetition is the repeated use of any element of language. This repetition helps to produce rhythm. One type of repetition is **parallelism**, the repeated use of words and phrases. In "Child of the Americas," the poets create a pattern by beginning each stanza with the phrase *I am.* This helps to link the parts of the poem.

Imagery refers to a poet's use of words to create mental pictures, or images. An image may appeal to any one of the five senses; for example, in "Child of the Americas," the phrase *the language of garlic and mangoes* appeals to the senses of smell and taste.

Another poetic device is **figurative language,** which uses figures of speech—ways of saying one thing to mean another. Simile and metaphor are two frequently used figures of speech. A **simile** compares two dissimilar objects, using *like* or *as,* as in "the rooster is early/Like a natural alarm" from "Poem." A **metaphor** is a comparison in which one thing is spoken of as though it were something else. For instance, in "Poem," Victor Hernandez Cruz uses the metaphor of the ocean for a person.

In the first group of poems in this unit, the poets tell how they see themselves. In the second group, the writers explore the experience of being a part of two different cultures. As you read each poem, pay careful attention to the writing devices each poet uses.

This realistic oil painting, entitled *Papiamento*, is by Julio Larraz, a well-known Cuban artist who came to the United States in 1961 to continue his art education. Larraz's love of the Caribbean is obvious; his painting provides vivid images of the beauty of the palm fronds, the figure of the woman, and the sparkling sun on the water. Larraz has lived in the Hudson Valley of New York as well as in Washington, D.C., and Miami, Florida. His work is found in numerous galleries and private collections of notable Latino art.

INTRODUCTION
Section 1: Identity

Each poem in this group expresses the poet's struggle to establish a sense of his or her own identity. Caught as they are between their Latino Caribbean heritage and the culture of the United States, the poets reveal their uncertainty about who they are.

In "Affirmations #3, Take Off Your Mask," Sandra María Esteves, a New York-born poet of Puerto Rican and Dominican heritage, instructs readers to cast aside their outward masks. She encourages them to look within themselves to discover their true identities. Gustavo Pérez Firmat was born in Havana, Cuba, and raised in Miami, Florida. In "Dedication," he tries to explain his feelings about writing in English rather than in Spanish. In "Child of the Americas," poet Aurora Levins Morales attempts to define herself in terms of her rich and varied ancestry. In "Migrating Notes," Josefina Báez speaks of the sense of division she feels as a Dominican living in the United States. Finally, in "You Call Me by Old Names," Rhina Espaillat states her preference for being called by names that reflect her present identity, not her past.

Affirmations #3, Take Off Your Mask

by Sandra María Esteves

Study the face behind it.
The one that has no flesh or bones.
The one that feels what the universe feels.

Take off the mask. Discard it.
Useless shell that it is.
An old skin. A cover.
Subject to weather distortions.[1]

See for yourself
the you inside no one else can see.

---

1. distortions (dihs-TAWR-shuhnz) *n. pl.* changes from the usual

Dedication

by Gustavo Pérez Firmat

The fact that I
am writing to you
in English
already falsifies what I
wanted to tell you.
My subject:
how to explain to you
that I
don't belong to English
though I belong nowhere else,
if not here
in English.

Child Of The Americas

by Aurora Levins Morales

I am a child of the Americas,
a light-skinned mestiza[1] of the Caribbean,
a child of many diaspora,[2] born into this continent at a
    crossroads.

I am a U.S. Puerto Rican Jew,
a product of the ghettos of New York I have never known.
An immigrant and the daughter and granddaughter of
    immigrants.
I speak English with passion: it's the tongue of my
    consciousness,
a flashing knife blade of crystal, my tool, my craft.

I am Caribeña, island grown. Spanish is in my flesh,
ripples from my tongue, lodges in my hips:
the language of garlic and mangoes,
the singing in my poetry, the flying gestures of my hands.
I am of Latinoamerica, rooted in the history of my
    continent:
I speak from that body.

---

1. **mestiza** (meh-STEE-zah) *n.* a woman of mixed European and
   Indian ancestry
2. **diaspora** (dy-AS-poh-ruh) *n.* the migration of a people

I am not african. Africa is in me, but I cannot return.
I am not taína.[3] Taíno is in me, but there is no way back.
I am not european. Europe lives in me, but I have no
    home there.

I am new. History made me. My first language was
    spanglish.[4]
I was born at the crossroads
and I am whole.

---

  3. taína (tah-EE-nah) *adj.* a woman of the Taíno, the native people of
    the Greater Antilles and the Bahamas
  4. spanglish (SPAN-glihsh) *n.* a mixture of Spanish and English

Migrating Notes

by Josefina Baez

I had no say in coming
I have illusions about going.

        Here I never belong
        about D.R. I just have a thought

memories of the past
create a false act

        Although very near
        It's not so clear.

Now bilingual   soul divided
Dominicanhood   strangely,   richly integrated
to this different and harsh reality
without realizing   rooting   aging.

You Call Me by Old Names

by Rhina Espaillat

You call me by old names: how strange
to think of "family" and "blood,"
walking through flakes, up to the knees
in cold and democratic mud.

And suddenly I think of people
dead many centuries ago:
my ancestors, who never knew
the dubious[1] miracle of snow. . . .

Don't say my names, you seem to mock
their charming, foolish, Old World touch.
Call me "immigrant," or Social
Security card such-and-such,

or future citizen, who boasts
two eyes, two ears, a nose, a mouth,
but no names from another life,
a long time back, a long way south.

---

1. dubious (DOO-bee-uhs) *adj.* doubtful

AFTER YOU READ

Exchanging Backgrounds and Cultures

1. In "Affirmations #3, Take Off Your Mask," what distinction does the speaker make between the outer and inner selves?

2. In "Dedication," "Child of the Americas," and "You Call Me by Old Names," what role does spoken or written language play in the way the speakers see themselves?

3. What illusions do you think the speaker of "Migrating Notes" has about going to the Dominican Republic? Which lines in the poem best support your conclusion?

What Do You Think?

Which poem or poems in this group did you find especially meaningful? What made them special?

Experiencing Poetry

The conflict between their Latino Caribbean heritage and their lives in the United States leaves the speakers of these poems struggling with their sense of identity. Think of an experience—your own or someone else's—involving a conflict that caused an inner struggle. Write a poem to express the feelings of struggle and what caused these feelings.

Optional Activity Write a poem that expresses your ideas about your first language or other languages you speak. In your poem, use parallelism to emphasize your main ideas. Remember, parallelism is the repetition of words and phrases to create a pattern, as Aurora Levins Morales did in "Child of the Americas."

INTRODUCTION

Section 2: Across Cultures

The four poets represented in this section explore the differences between what was familiar to them in their Latino Caribbean homelands and what they found when they came to the United States. In their poems, they remember the places that represent their cultural roots. Victor Hernández Cruz's "Poem" is filled with the rhythm of the music of the islands he knew as a young boy in Puerto Rico.

The next poem, "In My Country" by Ginetta E. Berloso Candelario, expresses the sadness and fear of the poor. Left without help from the upper and middle classes, their only hope is to leave their country for a new land.

In "Seeing Snow" by Gustavo Pérez Firmat, a Cuban American poet, the speaker feels uprooted. He expresses his continuing surprise at living in a place where there is snow. The last poem, "And Then Came . . . Freedom to Dream" by Puerto Rican poet Miguel Piñero, relates the immigrant's struggle to climb "the ladder called America" and become "100% AMERICAN."

Poem

by Victor Hernández Cruz

Your head it waves outside
You are as deep and heavy as the ocean
Night and day
Cabo Rojo[1]   the stars
Day and night
Arecibo[2] music in green
It rains   Rain washes coconuts
The mangos they fall off the trees
In midnights   You hear them falling
Sunshine   sol[3]
Your eyes they become one with the light
It is early   Early Early Early
And the rooster is early
Like a natural alarm
The music of the morning

Your head is full of the ocean and
The mystery of the sea shells
It moves like the waves

Moving outside the rhythms of life
Dawn birth deep in the mountains
Your eyes   they move
In and out of the woods
They look for spirits

---

1. **Cabo Rojo** (KAH-boh ROH-hoh) a small town in Puerto Rico
2. **Arecibo** (ahr-uh-SEE-boh) a city in Puerto Rico
3. **sol** (sohl) *n.* sun

Here is where our mothers are from
From this land sitting
All pregnant with sweetness
And trees that want to be the wind

Walking through the little space
The trees make
You want to laugh
In this lonely night there is music
And you do
And you don't stop
And the music is right behind you

Coquí[4]   Coquí   Coquí   Coquí

Here is where the journey started
And you laugh as tall as palm trees
And you taste as good as pasteles[5]
You dance toward the silver of the stars
Everything moves with you
Like a tropical train.

---

4. **Coquí** (koh-KEE) *n.* the sound made by the Coquí frog. The frog is
   found only in Puerto Rico.
5. **pasteles** (pahs-TEHL-ehs) *n. pl.* a traditional Puerto Rican dish
   consisting of bite-size pieces of meat wrapped inside a dough made
   of vegetables; similar to a Mexican tamale

In My Country

by Ginetta E. Berloso Candelario

. . . In my country
there is unity
women stick together
like just-fried plátanos maduros[1]
the product of women's work

In my country
women don't air their dirty laundry
only clean underwear hang from the fire escapes
the dirt collects by the hamper

In my country
well, in my country
there are fewer inhabitants each day
the raza[2] migrates to ivy towers, oak boardrooms,
porcelain-counter-topped kitchens,
leaving the rest of us behind
with only fearful backward glances
wondering if we might be trying to catch up with them
or if not, to reproduce against them

---

1. **plátanos maduros** (PLAH-tah-nohs mah-DOO-rohs) *n. pl.* ripe
   bananas
2. **raza** (RAH-sah) *n.* upper classes of society

Do you not recognize this beloved country of mine?
It is not in any atlas published by the "americanos"[3]
No, instead it is on the maps they give you for free
at the gas stations on I-95
the road we travel between
ayer y mañana[4]
vida y muerte[5]
esclavitud y libertad[6]
it is behind my eyes
and it is visible in the pallor[7] of my skin
when the blood drains from my face
at the sight of the graves of the U.S.A. muertos[8]
on I-95, as they ran from my country
to yours.

---

3. **americanos** (ah-meh-ree-KAH-nohs) *n. pl.* Americans
4. **ayer y mañana** (ah-YEHR ee mah-NYAH-nah) yesterday and tomorrow
5. **vida y muerte** (VEE-dah ee MWEHR-teh) life and death
6. **esclavitud y libertad** (ehs-klah-vee-TOOD ee lee-behr-TAHD) slavery and freedom
7. **pallor** (PAL-uhr) *adj.* paleness
8. **muertos** (MWEHR-tohs) *n. pl.* dead ones

Seeing Snow

by Gustavo Pérez Firmat

Had my father, my grandfather, and his,
had they been asked whether I would ever see snow,
they certainly—in another language—
would have answered,
no. Seeing snow for me
will always mean a slight or not so slight
suspension of the laws of nature.
I was not born to see snow.
I was not meant to see snow.
Even now, snowbound as I've been
all these years,
my surprise does not subside.
What, exactly, am I doing here?
Whose house is this anyway?
For sure one of us has strayed.
For sure someone's lost his way.
This must not be the place.
Where I come from, you know,
it's never snowed:
not once, not ever, not yet.

And Then Came...
Freedom to Dream

by Miguel Piñero

And then came
      one by one
      slow by slow
      left by right
      right by left
      word by word
      rung by rung
climbing the ladder called
        america

Me?
Well, I was going to try me
to see
if in me
      there was something
      that thing
      all men see
      but few possess
      that one thing
      that made the code
      we follow
      we struggle
      die for it
      die being it.

Then come the bravest
They . . . come . . . one by one . . .
Die that others may dream of reaching
       the top
       of the ladder
       and there close
       to Heaven
       is the next best thing
       for the pursuit of happiness
       for women & men
eternal roots—a symbol
of life lived in liberty
with a bathing of the spirit
       drenched in the
       earth
       sun
       rain
       moon rays
       light winds
       sounds of earth
       lowest creatures
       soil
       and land
       in the cradle of Rock & Roll
Disneyland,   Burger King, McDonald's
New York, New York—so nice they named it twice
of Menudo, Michael Jackson and Miami Vice
of being a Citizen of the
       greatest nation
       in the history of
       Man
       governing
       Man.

No words sound as pure as the
love in the smile
of an innocent child . .
Without reservation
without hesitation
Yes! . . . I Am . .
    100% AMERICAN
    YES . . . MISTER!!
Citizen of the UNITED
          STATES OF
          AMERICA!!

AFTER YOU READ

Exchanging Backgrounds and Cultures

1. In "Poem" and "In My Country," the poets combine English with Spanish words and phrases. What does this suggest about the poets' attitudes about being part of two cultures?

2. In "Seeing Snow," the poet uses the act of seeing snow as a metaphor for "not belonging." Why does the speaker have this feeling? What do you think he means by being "snowbound"?

3. In "And Then Came . . . Freedom to Dream," Miguel Piñero refers to "climbing the ladder called America." How does this image reflect the experience of immigrants?

What Do You Think?

Which poem in this group had a special impact on you? What effect did the poem as a whole have on you?

Experiencing Poetry

Miguel Piñero uses familiar images such as rock and roll, Disneyland, and Burger King as symbols of the United States. Write a poem that expresses your own ideas about the United States. In your poem, use names of places, people, or things that to *you* symbolize this country.

Optional Activity In "Seeing Snow," the speaker says that he has never gotten over his surprise at the sight of snow. Think about a natural event that surprises you whenever it occurs. Write a poem giving details about it and expressing your feelings at the time of the event.

UNIT 3: FOCUS ON WRITING

The message of a poem, as in other forms of literature, is conveyed through literary techniques, such as use of imagery and figurative language. What distinguishes poetry from other forms of literature is its musical quality, created through repetition, rhythm, and rhyme.

Writing a Poem

Consider the following topics: a special place, your favorite music, a person you admire, an event in the news. Then write a poem about one of these topics or another topic of your choice.

The Writing Process

Good writing requires both time and effort. An effective writer completes a number of stages that together make up the writing process. The stages of the writing process are given below to help guide you through your assignment.

Prewriting

After you have chosen a topic, create a list of images, or word pictures related to that topic. These images should appeal to the five senses: sight, hearing, touch, smell, and taste. For each of these senses, jot down as many images as you can that appeal to that sense. When you have finished, underline the most powerful images in your lists.

Next, think about the theme, or central message, you want to express. The images you include should relate to that theme. For example, in "Poem," Victor Hernández Cruz uses images of music and movement to evoke a tropical island.

Give some thought to the form of your poem. For instance, Miguel Piñero conveyed the image of a ladder by using a series of short lines resembling ladder rungs. Consider also whether your poem will have one stanza or several.

Think about how your poem will sound. Will you use a regular rhythm, or a pattern of accented syllables? Will you use rhyme or other sound devices, such as alliteration?

Drafting and Revising

As you begin drafting your poem, refer to your lists of images for ideas. Pay attention to how your poem sounds. You may want to pause after every few lines to read your poem aloud. Does it have the type of rhythm you planned to create?

After you have finished your first draft, read the entire poem aloud. It might help to set the poem aside for a while and then approach it with a fresh eye. Now is the time to note any lines or words that do not sound right or that fail to express exactly what you meant to say. Make any revisions you feel will improve your poem. It might be helpful to get a second opinion by reading the poem to a classmate.

Proofreading and Publishing

Now proofread your poem for errors in spelling, grammar, punctuation, and capitalization. Remember that in contemporary poetry, nonstandard punctuation and capitalization sometimes occur, so it is easy to overlook an error. Check any variation in your poem to make sure it is intentional.

Poetry is meant to be read aloud. You may want to hold a poetry reading in your class. Read your poem as expressively as possible, varying your volume and tone appropriately. You may want to submit your poem to the school newspaper or another publication for student writing.

UNIT 4
DRAMA OF THE LATINO CARIBBEANS

What sets drama apart from other literary forms is that it is meant to be seen and heard—to be performed. When you read a drama, try to picture in your mind how it would appear on the stage, on a television screen, or in a movie theater.

The format of drama is different from that of poems, stories, or novels. Drama is written so that the setting, the characters, and the characters' actions, emotions, and words can be clearly understood. **Stage directions** are the writer's instructions to the director and actors. They include descriptions of the scenery, props, costumes, lighting, and sound effects, as well as how the actors should speak and move. The words that each character speaks—the **dialogue**—are presented after the character's name.

Just as a novel is usually divided into chapters, a play is often divided into smaller sections, called **acts**. Within an act, there may be even smaller sections called **scenes**. You are about to read an excerpt from Miguel González-Pando's play *The Great American Justice Game,* which was written as one long act with four scenes.

González-Pando combines humor with historically correct information—major portions of the text spoken by the characters have been taken from actual speeches and documents. His hope in writing this play was to amuse and entertain audiences. But he also hoped to make people think seriously about the play's subject and theme. As you read the play, try to picture the setting and the characters, and imagine how the events unfold onstage.

Adolfo Piantini, born in the Dominican Republic in 1946, was trained both in New York and in the Dominican Republic. Now living in Miami, Florida, he has had many major exhibits of his work throughout the United States and the Caribbean. *In Cayenas*, a 1978 work that combines acrylic paint and collage, Piantini presents two young girls. Notice the flowers in one girl's hand and on the other girl's skirt, images of the artist's life in the Dominican Republic.

INTRODUCTION

The Great American Justice Game

Miguel González-Pando (mee-GWEHL gohn-SAHL-es PAHN-doh) was born in Cuba in 1941. He was exiled from his homeland twice, once in 1958 when he fought against the government of Fulgencio Batista and again in 1960 after Fidel Castro took control of Cuba. González-Pando was captured after he took part in the U.S.-backed invasion of Cuba in 1961, and was sentenced to a 30-year prison term. He was released and returned to the United States in 1962 as part of a settlement between Cuba and the United States.

González-Pando settled in Miami, where he has taken an active part in political, educational, and civil rights issues related to the Latino community. Through its humor, his play *The Great American Justice Game* speaks out against those who would deny freedom of expression to all people. In his play, González-Pando speaks in the name of all underrepresented groups. As a playwright, he draws upon his immigrant background, his political experiences, and his interest in people who are oppressed. He uses his artistic talents to be a "voice" of the oppressed and to make a difference in their lives.

from *The Great American Justice Game*

by Miguel González-Pando

Characters

LIBERTY, . . . Latin woman in a Statue of Liberty costume.
She represents the conscience of America. She speaks
only to the audience, as the other characters can
neither see nor hear her.

JUDGE, . . . man with Spanish accent and exaggerated
mannerisms,[1] wearing heavy makeup. He doubles as
judge in the trial and host of the game show, speaking
through a megaphone, and switching from mocking
pomposity[2] to outright irreverence.[3]

BAILIFF, fat man with German accent who affects childish
attitudes. He represents the simpleminded fanatic.[4]

MARIA, pretty fifteen-year-old girl with blonde hair and blue
eyes. Defendant in the trial. She represents the victims
of the supra-ethnic[5] American nation as well as its
hope for the future.

---

1. **mannerisms** (MAN-uhr-ihz-uhmz) *n. pl.* special manners or ways
   of doing something that have become a habit
2. **pomposity** (pahm-PAHS-uh-tee) *n.* self-important behavior
3. **irreverence** (ih-REHV-uhr-uhns) *n.* lack of respect for religion or
   things that deserve respect
4. **simpleminded fanatic** (SIHM-puhl-meyend-ihd fuh-NAT-ihk) a
   foolish person with an unreasonable amount of zeal or enthusiasm
5. **supra-ethnic** (SOO-pruh-ETH-nik) *adj.* having a great deal of cultural diversity

DEFENSE, articulate old man of weak character, concerned
    with formal legal procedures rather than justice. He
    represents the established order.
PROSECUTOR, passionate man with a strong personality. He
    represents bigotry.
CHORUS, composed of at least eight to ten actors,
    representing the mindless masses whose role in society
    is confined to being an echo. In a small production,
    the chorus may also be played by the celebrity
    witnesses, in which case they will move around the
    stage, but remain in semi-darkness until called upon
    individually to testify.
CELEBRITY WITNESSES, Founding Father, Noble Savage,
    Uncle Tom, White Supremacist, and Superman.

The action takes place circa 2005.

SCENE 1

The stage is dark. A dim light begins to shine over a . . . woman dressed as the Statue of Liberty. The light grows more intense as she speaks in a heavy Spanish accent. Chorus humming "America the Beautiful" in the background.

LIBERTY: . . ."Give me your tired, your poor,
　　　　　Your huddled masses yearning to breathe free,
　　　　　The wretched refuse of your teeming shore.
　　　　　Send these, the homeless, tempest-tost to me,
　　　　　I lift my lamp beside the golden door."—
　　　　　You know?

The music slowly gets out of tune, quick blackout.

JUDGE: Show time, show time, ladies and gentlemen, come in please! Show time, show time! What? Yes, the girls are inspected, but don't drink the water! Ha ha ha . . .

BAILIFF: (*Blowing a whistle.*) Silence! Silence! Hear ye, hear ye, this court is now in session. Honorable Fair N. Square presiding. And now, here comes the judge!

Curtains open. Set looks like that of a typical game show. From left to right: seating for the defense attorney, the defendant, the judge, the witness, the bailiff, and the prosecutor.

CHORUS: (*While Judge puts on his robe.*)
　　　　　"Here comes the judge, here comes the judge,
　　　　　clap your hands and rise to your feet

'cause he's Fair N. Square and he's got that beat.
Here comes the judge, here comes the judge,
clap your hands and rise to your feet
justice's coming with all deliberate speed."

JUDGE: Thank you, thank you, Bailiff. (*To the audience.*) Are you ready to play "The Great American Justice Game"? (*Using the megaphone.*) Bailiff, will you introduce today's contestants?

BAILIFF: The first contestant, representing the defense, is a full-blooded American, and his favorite pastime is watching old Perry Mason movies. And, our second contestant, representing the prosecution, can trace his ancestry all the way back to the Mayflower.

JUDGE: Let's give a fine round of applause to both of these one hundred percent Americans who will decide the fate of today's defendant in "The Great American Justice Game." And now, let's get ready to play! (*Suddenly turning pompous.*) Bring the defendant in! (*María Libertad, gagged, is brought in.*) Will the Bailiff read the charges!

BAILIFF: The defendant, María Libertad, is charged with the use of a foreign language in public, in violation of the English and English Only Act, which prescribes that English and English only shall be spoken in these United States. The defendant has continued to speak Spanish since she was found alone hiding in a cave deep within the Rocky Mountains. Furthermore, she has ignored all attempts to communicate with her in English.

JUDGE: (*Using the megaphone.*) And how does the defendant plead?

DEFENSE: I am entering a plea of nolo contendere . . .[6]

BAILIFF: (*Blowing the whistle.*) English! English only!

---

6. **nolo contendere** (NOH-loh kuhn-TEHN-duh-reh) from the Latin, a plea by the defendant that, without admitting guilt, does not deny the charges; literally, "I do not wish to contend."

CHORUS: English! English only!

DEFENSE: I am sorry, Your Honor; I mean "no contest." We plead no contest because the defendant never had an opportunity to learn English. She was born in the cave where her parents went into hiding when the English and English Only Act became law. Her parents, Your Honor, joined the massive exodus of Spanish speakers who decided to go underground rather than give up their language, and they taught her only Spanish.

PROSECUTOR: Your Honor, will you remind the defense that ignorance of the English language does not justify the use of any other language.

JUDGE: Five points under the category of "Put up or shut up" for the contestant for the prosecution, who takes an early lead! (*Using the megaphone.*) The defense is so reminded.

DEFENSE: I am not trying to justify anything, Your Honor—just explaining the facts: that the defendant, never having been taught English, could not help but speak Spanish.

PROSECUTOR: And how has the attorney for the defense come to know those facts? Did he communicate in Spanish with the defendant, Miss Libertad—or did she draw him a picture?

JUDGE: Five more points for the contestant for the prosecution under the category of "A picture is not worth a single English word!" The contestant for the prosecution now leads by ten points!

DEFENSE: Me use Spanish! Of course not! Being a law-abiding citizen, I have been careful not to discuss this case with the defendant. In fact, when I met María Libertad at the English and English Only Enforcement Agency, I asked the guards to gag her, and even then, as an additional precaution, I wore earmuffs, just in case . . . I can assure you, Your Honor, that no communication whatsoever has been established between the defendant and myself.

JUDGE: Those extreme precautions are worth ten points to the contestant for the defense . . . ! And so, with the score even at ten points, we now have a tie game!

LIBERTY: This is a mockery of justice! A circus! You know? Is this what you call due process?[7]

JUDGE: Since the contestant for the defense entered the plea of no contest, we will not be concerned with determining whether María Libertad is innocent or guilty. The question here is what would be an appropriate sentence—if she is found guilty, as certainly appears to be the case. Therefore, I want both contestants to address the issue of punishment in their opening statements.

PROSECUTOR: Your Honor, the English and English Only Act is clear and unequivocal:[8] the defendant's insistence upon using Spanish, whether by choice or necessity, makes her guilty, and the sentence dictated by the law is her sterilization and commitment for life to a permanent detention center for hardcore speakers of foreign languages. There she shall remain isolated from society in order to ensure that her language and her ways do not contaminate this great nation of ours.

BAILIFF: Sterilize her! Sterilize her! (*Blowing the whistle.*) Let me do it!

CHORUS: Sterilize her! Sterilize her!

DEFENSE: Your Honor, María Libertad is merely a teenager. She needs to be rehabilitated, to be taught English. She can be naturalized and Americanized—it's still not too late for her.

---

7. **due process** (DOO PRAW-sehs) legal proceedings carried out in accordance with established rules and procedures

8. **unequivocal** (un-ih-KWIHV-uh-kuhl) *adj.* very clear in meaning; plain

LIBERTY: How can we discuss punishment before determining if the defendant is guilty or innocent, damn it! Besides, the defendant must be presumed innocent until proven guilty! María Libertad has the right to a fair trial, you know?

PROSECUTOR: Your Honor, the prosecution is prepared to introduce evidence showing that María Libertad is too old to undergo naturalization and Americanization. She will always remain a threat to our society unless she is sterilized and committed to the isolated environment of a permanent detention center.

BAILIFF: Sterilize her and cut her tongue off!

CHORUS: Sterilize her and cut her tongue off!

PROSECUTOR: I have here the record of thousands of documented cases of Spanish-speaking adolescents who were given the opportunity to participate in rehabilitation programs to become naturalized and Americanized. They did, of course, learn English, but consistently refused to forget their native language. At best, Your Honor, the defendant may become bilingual—and bilingualism is an even greater threat!

CHORUS: Bilingualism is an even greater threat!

JUDGE: That argument is worth five more points. . . . The contestant for the prosecution has again retaken a five-point lead!

PROSECUTOR: Thank you, Your Honor. I insist that María Libertad poses a serious threat to our society. Even if she could master the English language, we are responsible for ensuring that she would not teach Spanish secretly to others—to her children, for example. The law is clear, Your Honor: the defendant must be sterilized and remain isolated for the rest of her wretched life.

BAILIFF: Sterilize her! Sterilize her!

CHORUS: Sterilize her! Sterilize her!

PROSECUTOR: Need I remind this court how obstinate

and sneaky these people are . . . the stubbornness with
which they cling to their language and their ways? Just
look how they reacted to the passage of the English and
English Only Act: the very fact that millions of Spanish
speakers deserted their jobs and abandoned their
homes to take their families into hiding shows how
dangerous these people can be.

JUDGE: Good! Five more points to the contestant for the
prosecution . . . ! The contestant for the prosecution
now leads the game by ten points.

DEFENSE: Your Honor, "these people" are not on trial—
María Libertad is the only one on trial here! This girl
cannot be tried as the reincarnation of those . . . "Frito
Banditos"[9] who under the guise of cultural pluralism[9]
once threatened to change America. Just look at her,
Your Honor; does she seem dangerous to you? She
even looks American—the girl is blonde and has blue
eyes, for God's sake, Your Honor!

JUDGE: I'm going to award ten full points to the
contestant for the defense under the category of
"Wrapping yourself with the American flag"! We again
have a tie game! (*A loud horn blows.*) Oops! Do you
know what that horn means? It means that now, the
other contestant has only six seconds to blow the "horn
of justice" and send this game into overtime! Bailiff,
hand the horn of justice to the contestant for the
prosecution and start counting!

BAILIFF: (*Chorus repeats each number.*) Six . . . five . . . four
. . . three . . . two . . . one . . . (*Prosecutor blows the horn.*)

JUDGE: Good! With one second left the contestant for the
prosecution beat the clock! Well, do you have a good
counterargument to the "Wrap yourself with the

---

9. **cultural pluralism** (KUHL-chur-uhl PLOOR-uhl-ihz-uhm) the main-
taining of separate traditions by diverse ethnic and racial groups
within the confines of a common civilization

American flag" appeal used by the contestant for the defense?

PROSECUTOR: I certainly do. Since the defense has appealed to our pride in America, Your Honor, I will call as my first celebrity witness none other than Mr. Founding Father himself.

JUDGE: That's a tremendous move by the contestant for the prosecution, sending the game into overtime! So, with the score even at twenty points, it will be his turn next to question the celebrity witness—but first, let's hear a word or two from our commercial sponsors, the people who make all this possible. Don't go away, 'cause we'll be right back to continue playing "The Great American Justice Game"! Studio audience, watch that monitor. . .

Black out and cut to pre-taped TV commercial.

COMMERCIAL *(Like in the Rolaids commercial.)*

REPORTER: We are now standing on the steps of the United Nations. They have just concluded a lengthy session, and we'll try to catch the American ambassador as he gets ready to leave. (*Looks around.*) Here comes Ambassador Hayakawa, the former senator from the state of California—let's see if he wants to say a few words. (*Calling Ambassador Hayakawa.*) Ambassador! Ambassador Hayakawa! (*Ambassador Hayakawa walks over.*) Ambassador, how do you spell "relief"?

AMBASSADOR: E-n-g-l-i-s-h: English! That's how I spell "relief . . . "

REPORTER: That's right folks, nothing takes the edge off a rough day of listening to the constant chatter of loud Spanish better than the soft and soothing sound of English. So . . . when you've had a long day full of "oye," "mira," "qué pasa," and "hola,"[10] come back to

---

10. oye (OH-yeh) *v.* hear; **mira** (MEE-rah) *v.* look; **qué pasa** (keh PAH-sah) what's happening; **hola** (OH-lah) *interj.* hello

the only language that full-blooded Americans understand: English!

AMBASSADOR: E-n-g-l-i-s-h: English! That's how I spell "relief..."

VOICE OVER: English, void where prohibited by practice: places like the United Nations and most foreign countries.

SCENE 2

JUDGE: Welcome back to "The Great American Justice Game"! Our score is tied at twenty points apiece. And now, let's continue playing. (*Using the megaphone.*) If the contestant for the prosecution is ready, we'll call his first celebrity witness.

BAILIFF: (*Blowing the whistle.*) Mr. Founding Father, come to the stand! (*To the judge, as Founding Father comes forward.*) Your Honor, look at his hair—it's long and curly. He's wearing a wig! I want a pretty wig like that too! I want a long and curly wig!

JUDGE: Bailiff! Will you stop that nonsense and swear in the witness! (*To Founding Father.*) I must apologize for the bailiff's weird behavior, Mr. Founding Father...

BAILIFF: (*Handing the witness a copy of* Webster's New English Dictionary.) Place your left hand on this copy of *Webster's New English Dictionary* and close your right eye. Do you solemnly swear that the testimony you are about to give will be in English, wholly in English, and in nothing but English, so help you Webster?

WITNESS: Cross my heart and hope to die!

CHORUS: Cross my heart and hope to die!

BAILIFF: (*Curiously staring at the wig.*) Be seated!

JUDGE: (*Using the megaphone.*) The contestant for

the prosecution can now begin questioning his celebrity witness.

PROSECUTOR: Thank you, Your Honor. As one of the Founding Fathers, do you believe that our government has the right—indeed, the responsibility—to defend our values, our ways and, especially, our language, from anyone threatening to change this great land of ours? And please, don't hesitate to dispense with the customary egalitarian[11] rhetoric . . .

FOUNDING FATHER: We didn't make the American Revolution to let our nation become undermined by people of different languages, different ways, and different colors. It is an established historical fact that most of my fellow Founding Fathers felt torn between the American ideals of liberty and equality, on the one hand, and the more practical considerations of the time, on the other—if you know what I mean. Benjamin Franklin, of course, never having owned slaves, could well indulge in dreaming about extending full equality to all . . .

JUDGE: That answer is worth five points under the category of "Do as we preach, but not as we do" for the contestant for the prosecution, who again leads the game by the score of twenty-five to twenty!

LIBERTY: . . . And what about those rousing words of the Declaration of Independence: "We hold these truths to be self-evident, that all men are created equal, that they are endowed by their Creator with certain unalienable[12] Rights, that among these are Life, Liberty and the pursuit of Happiness"! You know?

---

11. **egalitarian** (ih-gal-uh-TEHR-ee-uhn) *adj.* marked by a belief in human equality
12. **unalienable** (un-AYL-yuh-nuh-buhl) *adj.* incapable of being surrendered or transferred

136

DEFENSE: Your Honor, with all due respect to the witness, his testimony must be placed within its proper perspective. We must remember that those were other times, that the Founding Fathers faced a different historical moment. Why, none other than our first president, George Washington himself, was a slaveholder. And so was Jefferson, the egalitarian author of the Declaration of Independence, whose views on Blacks and Indians certainly excluded them from consideration as equals. And who, Your Honor, would dare question these men's ideals? Who would dare question their patriotism?

LIBERTY: The defense's argument is unacceptable! What is morally abhorrent[13] today, was also morally abhorrent in 1776. The weight of the historical evidence should clearly speak to America's collective conscience. The defense is making a mockery of America's judicial system! You know?

PROSECUTOR: (*To the witness.*) Then, based upon your recollections of the real intentions of the Founding Fathers, it is your expert opinion that they would have supported the English and English Only Act, right?

FOUNDING FATHER: Absolutely . . . you see, the Founding Fathers were realistic men of a practical nature—the Declaration of Independence notwithstanding. Besides, it is well recognized that all nations have the right to dictate the language which is to be spoken by their citizens within their borders. Let me put it this way: we have as much right to dictate that only English be spoken in America as, for example, Méjico[14] has to require Spanish within its territory.

---

13. **abhorrent** (uhb-HAWR-uhnt) *adj.* causing fear, disgust, or hatred
14. **Méjico** (MEH-hee-koh) Mexico

Why, can you imagine anyone questioning the right of the Mexican government to dictate the use of Spanish in . . . let's say . . . Nuevo Méjico?

JUDGE: A point of clarification: Nuevo Méjico is no longer pronounced Nuevo Méjico—it is now pronounced New Mexico. (*Using the megaphone.*) New Mexico has been under the control of the United States since we took it from Mexico in 1848, and of course, Spanish has not been allowed to be spoken there since the passage of the English and English Only Act!

FOUNDING FATHER: No kidding . . . well, then what about Tejas? Doesn't the Mexican government have the sovereign[15] right, if it so chooses, to dictate that Spanish be the only language of Tejas?

JUDGE: I beg your pardon, Mr. Founding Father, but Tejas is no longer pronounced Tejas—it is now pronounced Texas, and English is the official language there today. Oh, and of course, (*Using the megaphone.*) Texas has been part of these United States since 1845. Remember the Alamo?

CHORUS: Remember the Alamo!

FOUNDING FATHER: Well, can you then imagine anyone questioning the right of the Mexican government to require only Spanish in their territory of . . . California!

JUDGE: Mr. Founding Father, I am sorry, but I must inform you that California is no longer under the jurisdiction of the Mexican government. It has belonged to the United States since 1848; therefore, Spanish is no longer allowed there. (*Using the megaphone.*) English is now the only language allowed in California!

FOUNDING FATHER: Is that so . . . ? Well, can you then imagine anyone questioning the right of the Spanish

---

15. **sovereign** (SAHV-ruhn) *adj.* independent; not controlled by others

government to insist that only Spanish be spoken in its territory of La Florida?

JUDGE: Again, I must correct you: La Florida is no longer pronounced La Florida—it is now pronounced Florida, and it ceased being a Spanish colony in 1819, when it became part of the United States. (*Using the megaphone.*) English is the only language spoken in . . .

FOUNDING FATHER: And how about the other territories that were first discovered by the Spaniards—what about Arizona, Nevada, Utah, Alabama, Colorado, Mississippi, and Oklahoma? Has the Spanish language also been banned from those territories?

JUDGE: I am afraid so! (*Using the megaphone.*) America is no longer composed of just thirteen small colonies. We have taken over all the territory from Canada in the north to the Rio Grande in the south. And of course, the United States also governs Alaska, Hawaii, the Virgin Islands, and Puerto Rico. Cha-cha-cha!

CHORUS: Cha-cha-cha!

FOUNDING FATHER: Alaska! The Russians do not own Alaska?

JUDGE: No, no, no, no, no, no . . .

CHORUS: No, no, no, no, no, no . . .

FOUNDING FATHER: Well, and what about Louisiana? Louisiana is still French, is it not?

JUDGE: I beg your pardon, but again, I must correct you: Louisiana is not French anymore. (*Using the megaphone.*) Louisiana is now part of the United States, and English is the only language spoken there today. And yes, let me add that Montana, Wyoming, the Dakotas, Nebraska, Iowa, Arkansas, Minnesota, Oklahoma, Missouri, and all the other North American territories that once belonged to France, also became part of the United States in 1803! Oh-la-la!

CHORUS: Oh-la-la!

FOUNDING FATHER: Are you telling me that the

children of the children who once spoke Russian in Alaska, and French in Louisiana and all the Mississippi Valley, as well as those who once spoke Spanish in La Florida, Tejas, California, Arizona, Nevada, Colorado, Kansas, Utah, Nuevo Méjico, Puerto Rico, and parts of Alabama and Mississippi, are you telling me that now they are only allowed to speak English?

JUDGE: That's correct! (*Using the megaphone.*) The English and English Only Act is the supreme law of the land!

CHORUS: The English and English Only Act is the supreme law of the land!

FOUNDING FATHER: And the Indians? All those tribes which once roamed free, have they also been forced to give up their native languages?

JUDGE: (*Using the megaphone.*) Mr. Founding Father, I have just told you—repeatedly—that English and English only is allowed in the United States!

FOUNDING FATHER: Well, in that case, then . . . never mind . . .

JUDGE: I am sorry, but we must deduct five points from the score of the contestant for the prosecution, since his witness' testimony failed to support his case. So now the game is again tied at twenty points! Cha-cha-cha! (*Chorus repeats "cha-cha-cha."*) The contestant for the defense can now call his first celebrity witness.

LIBERTY: The forefathers of the defendant María Libertad not only brought the Spanish language when they settled in parts of La Florida, California, Tejas, Arizona, Alabama, Colorado, Kansas, Utah, Nuevo Méjico, and Puerto Rico, but by the time that the pilgrims landed at Plymouth Rock, the Spaniards had already established five universities, several printing presses, and hundreds of churches and schools in those territories which later became part of the United States. You know? . . .

Black out and cut to pre-taped TV commercial.

COMMERCIAL

ANNOUNCER: Remember those old movie classics that you enjoyed as a child? Movies like *Gone with the Wind, Fiddler on the Roof, Westside Story,* and other all-time favorites?

Well, now you can increase your viewing pleasure! That's right, you can now watch your favorite movies again and again without having to sit through those bothersome scenes showing Blacks, Jews, Puerto Ricans, and other minorities who are not one hundred percent Americans. . . .

So, bring your family together . . . and get ready to really enjoy *Gone with the Wind* with an all-white cast, *Fiddler on the Roof* without crooked noses, or *Westside Story* in perfect English . . . How sweet it is!

VOICE OVER: WASPish Movie Classics, now available exclusively through . . . retail stores right in your own neighborhood. . . .

SCENE 4

JUDGE: Welcome back again to "The Great American Justice Game"! As we begin the final segment of our show, the contestant for the prosecution is ahead by the score of thirty to twenty. Obviously, the fate of today's defendant, María Libertad, is beginning to look very bad. But now, the contestant for the defense will get a chance to call his last celebrity witness. (*Using the megaphone.*) Is the contestant for the defense ready?

DEFENSE: Yes, Your Honor. As my last celebrity witness I want to call a man who is faster than a speeding bullet . . .

JUDGE: . . . (*To the defense.*) Will the contestant for the defense please identify his witness? Cha-cha-chaa!

CHORUS: Cha-cha-chaa!

DEFENSE: Your Honor, I am, of course, referring to Superman!

JUDGE: (*Using the megaphone.*) Bailiff, please call Superman to the stand.

BAILIFF: (*Blowing the whistle.*) Superman, come to the stand! (*Handing Superman a book.*) Place your left hand on this copy of *Webster's New English Dictionary* and close your right eye. Do you solemnly swear that the testimony you are about to give will be in English, wholly in English, and in nothing but English, so help you Webster?

SUPERMAN: Cross my heart and hope to die!

CHORUS: Cross my heart and hope to die!

JUDGE: The contestant for the defense may now proceed to question his witness . . .

DEFENSE: Thank you, Your Honor. Superman, I have only one question for you: how many languages do you speak?

SUPERMAN: Well, it's hard to tell, but my adventures are told in more than a dozen languages to people from approximately one hundred countries—that's what makes me the most universal of all American heroes. Of course, having been born on the planet Krypton, my native language is really Kryptonian.

DEFENSE: There you are, Your Honor! The man who stands as a universal symbol of freedom, justice, and the American way of life, has just testified that he speaks more than a dozen languages and that his native tongue is not even English, but Kryptonian!

PROSECUTOR: I object, Your Honor! I object! The testimony of this witness should be stricken from the record on the grounds that Superman is really an illegal alien!

JUDGE: Objection sustained! The witness is excused!

BAILIFF: But I like Superman . . .

JUDGE: Well, this game . . . I mean . . . trial is quickly approaching its conclusion, and since there are no more witnesses, it's time now for both contestants to present their final arguments, which can be worth up to twenty full points. First, the contestant for the prosecution will get his chance to deliver the closing statement.

PROSECUTOR: My fellow Americans, we are God's chosen people! In 1789, America was limited to just thirteen states, but we responded to the Anglo-Saxon calling within us and the march of the American way of life swept from ocean to ocean until God's chosen people could, in time, celebrate that the Indians became civilized and the Blacks were emancipated and the Hispanics were taught English—and they all were given the opportunity to participate in the American way of life.

CHORUS: (*Singing.*) And the march of the American way went on and on!

LIBERTY: (*Over the humming of the Chorus.*) My God, how can we forget the contributions which each of those groups has made to the development of America? There need not be a conflict between being Indian or Black or Hispanic, and also being American! You know?

CHORUS: (*Marching and singing.*) And the march of the American way went on and on!

PROSECUTOR: (*Over the humming of the Chorus.*) And then, despite the constant triumphal march of the American way of life, our destiny was challenged, not by the enemies beyond our borders, but challenged from within, challenged by those . . . whose misery we replaced with America's plenty, and whose chaos and tyranny were swept away by the highest honor liberty can bestow: citizenship in the great American Republic!

CHORUS: (*Again marching and singing.*) And the march of the American way went on and on!

PROSECUTOR: (*Over the humming of the Chorus.*) Those . . . immigrants, illegal aliens, refugees, . . . made attempts against the American way of life as God has revealed it, threatening our traditions, our language, and our culture.

CHORUS: (*Marching and singing.*) And the march of the American way went on and on!

PROSECUTOR: (*Over the humming of the Chorus.*) The girl on trial today for violating the English and English Only Act represents the reincarnation[16] of that threat. She is the enemy, and her language and culture are her deadly weapons. Make no mistake about it. Anything but the full sentence prescribed by the law would signal that our faith in the American way has weakened. It would be an invitation for the resurgence of cultural pluralism and bilingualism, not to mention the return of the Mexican taco, the Cuban sandwich . . . !

CHORUS: (*Marching and singing in crescendo.*) And the march of the American way went on and on!

PROSECUTOR: (*Over the humming of the Chorus.*) My fellow Americans, as God's chosen people we cannot shrink from our sacred duties, for it is ours to execute the fate that has driven us to be greater than any other nation. We cannot allow any retreat from the path that leads to the fulfillment of God's manifest destiny, and that destiny is written in the English language and only in the English language!

---

16. **reincarnation** (ree-ihn-kahr-NAY-shuhn) *n.* reappearance after death in a new body

CHORUS: (*Concluding the marching song.*) And the march of the American way went on and on! And the march of the American way went on and on!

JUDGE: Hallelujah! That closing statement is worth the full twenty points for the contestant for the prosecution, who continues increasing his lead.

LIBERTY: . . . How in God's name can we justify putting limits on man's expression as a leash is put on a dog . . . and then pretend that we have changed their nature? To restrict the freedom of expression of just one girl is to question the spontaneous manifestation of life itself. To impose a common denominator, be it a uniform language or a homogenized culture, is to brutalize our senses and to cry out against the very miracle of creation. You know? Ladies and gentlemen, let's stand up and cheer: "Vive la différence!"[17]

CHORUS: Vive la différence!

JUDGE: And now we will hear the closing statement from the contestant for the defense.

DEFENSE: The English and English Only Act of 1990, Your Honor, does not appear to take into account that in English the word "language" has two different meanings, which are so distinct as to provoke semantic[18] ambiguity.[19] In one interpretation, the word has a plural (namely, languages) and may be preceded by the definite or indefinite article. The other interpretation has no plural, and is never preceded by any article.

PROSECUTOR: I object, Your Honor! The defense's argument is not only irrelevant, but also difficult to follow . . .

---

17. **Vive la différence** (VEEV LAH dee-fay-RAWNS) French expression meaning long live differentness
18. **semantic** (suh-MAN-tihk) *adj.* having to do with the study of the meanings of words
19. **ambiguity** (am-buh-GYOO-uh-tee) *n.* the condition of being unclear or indefinite

JUDGE: Objection sustained! The contestant for the defense loses five points and is risking disqualification if his closing statement does not address the issues of this trial in a more relevant manner!

LIBERTY: The fundamental issue here is freedom of expression, which is the cornerstone of America! I never thought that this would come to pass! You know! (*Crying.*) God, why has the American dream become a nightmare?

CHORUS: Why has the American dream become a nightmare?

DEFENSE: Your Honor, such morphological[20] and syntactic[21] distinctions are indeed relevant since they have semantic implications. When referring to "a language," one means a conventional system of speech practiced throughout a rather extensive community, such as English or Latin. Those are "languages" in the popular meaning of the term. To refer to "language," however, is to speak of something much broader. In what sense "much broader"? Well, in the same sense as "I like dancing" is to make a much broader statement than "I like this type of dance," when speaking, for example, of the waltz. Dancing, broadly speaking, may indeed by to my liking—although I may dislike a particular dance . . .

LIBERTY: My God! I can't believe that this is happening in America! What kind of defense argument is that? A girl's life is being decided, and the defense, all of a sudden, gets the urge to go dancing! You know? This whole trial has been a Mickey Mouse affair!

CHORUS: A Mickey Mouse affair! (*Singing the Mickey Mouse Mouseketeers' song.*) M—I—C—K—E—Y, M—O—U—S—E . . . Mickey Mouse, Mickey Mouse . . .

---

20. morphological (mawr-fuh-LAHJ-ih-kuhl) *adj.* having to do with the study of parts and forms of words

21. syntactic (sihn-TAK-tihk) *adj.* having to do with the way in which words are put together to form phrases, clauses, or sentences

(*The Chorus gets excited and sings the Mouseketeer's song louder and louder.*)

JUDGE: Order! Order! (*Raps the gavel three times.*)

Quick blackout: at this point there is complete silence for an instant, then the rapping of the gavel is heard again as if someone were knocking on a door. A spotlight begins shining on María Libertad, who seems to be sleeping.

LIBERTY: Mickey . . . Mickey Mouse . . . ! (*Off stage, as if she were calling María Libertad.*)

MARIA: (*Waking up, alarmed and confused.*) Mickey Mouse! Mickey Mouse!

LIBERTY: (*Enters.*) But María, you've fallen asleep and haven't put on the Mickey Mouse costume yet! Come on, hurry up! We're going to be late for the Halloween party . . . You know?

MARIA: Mamá, Mamá! I had an awful dream! A nightmare!

LIBERTY: Come on, hurry up! Your father's already dressed up and waiting! You know? You should see him—he looks so proud wearing his Ponce de León costume! (*To the public.*) Wow . . . I bet that tonight his is going to sing me those old Spanish songs that drive me . . .

MARIA: (*Hysterical, interrupting her mother.*) Mamá, Mamá! I dreamed that we could no longer speak Spanish—that it was illegal—and that I was involved in this horrible trial because . . . It was awful, Mamá, it was so awful . . .

LIBERTY: María, cálmate[22] . . . You were just dreaming, baby . . . You don't have to be afraid . . . This is America, you know, the land of the free!

Chorus begins humming "America the Beautiful."

MARIA: But Mamá, it all seemed so real!

---

22. cálmate (KAHL-mah-teh) *v.* calm down

LIBERTY: Mi amor, estamos en América![23] That could never happen here . . . You know? It was just a bad nightmare . . . Ven, déjame darte un beso.[24] (*They embrace.*)

MARIA: (*Beginning to relax.*) And you were also in my nightmare, Mamá—wearing your Statue of Liberty costume . . .

LIBERTY: . . . Then for sure my Ponce de León will sing me the old Spanish songs tonight. . . .

MARIA: Mamá, qué bueno que somos americanos![25] I am so proud to be an American! (*Stage lights come on again as Mariá puts on the Mouseketeers' ears and runs to take the megaphone away from the Judge; then she yells to the audience.*) I'm so proud to be an American! Give me an "A"!

CHORUS: "A!"

MARIA: Give me an "M!"

CHORUS: "M!"

MARIA: Give me an "E!"

CHORUS: "E!"

MARIA: Give me an "R!"

CHORUS: "R!"

MARIA: Give me an "I!"

CHORUS: "I!"

MARIA: Give me a "C!"

CHORUS: "C!"

MARIA: Give me an "A!"

CHORUS: "A!"

---

23. **Mi amor, estamos en América!** (mee ah-MOHR ehs-TAH-mohs ehn ah-MEH-ree-kah) My love, we are in America!
24. **Ven, dejame darte un beso.** (vehn deh-HAH-meh DAHR-teh oon BEH-soh) Come, give me a kiss.
25. **qué bueno que somos americanos!** (keh BWEH-noh keh soh-MOHS ah-meh-ree-KAH-nohs) How good it is that we are Americans!

MARIA: Give me a "U!"
CHORUS: "U!"
MARIA: Give me an "S!"
CHORUS: "S!"
MARIA: Give me an "A!"
CHORUS: "A!"
MARIA: And, what do you get!
CHORUS: *Singing to the Mouseketeers' tune, the entire cast joins
in singing and parading with great joy. Fireworks go off, and
red, white, and blue balloons are released into the audience.)*

> A–M–E–R–I–C–A for U–S–A!
> U–S–A! U–S–A!
> Where freedom and justice does prevail!
> A–M–E–R–I–C–A for U–S–A!
> U–S–A . . . U–S–A
> The land of hope and faith!
> A–M–E–R–I–C–A for U–S–A!
> U–S–A! U–S–A!

Blackout. Curtain falls.

AFTER YOU READ

Exchanging Backgrounds and Cultures

1. In the play, many Spanish speakers went into hiding rather than give up their language. What does this reveal about their attitude toward their heritage?

2. The prosecutor refers to María's language and culture as "deadly weapons." How might one person's language and culture threaten another person's?

3. Do you think that an English and English Only Act could ever really become the law of the United States? Why or why not?

What Do You Think?

Which character or scene in the play was most meaningful to you? Why?

Experiencing Drama

In this play, González-Pando uses a game show format to make fun of the trial of a young girl accused of speaking Spanish. How might the play have been different if written as serious drama? Choose a brief scene from the play and rewrite it in a serious tone.

Optional Activity Write a scene based on a political issue or trial that is currently in the news. Remember to provide stage directions that describe the setting, and include dialogue for your characters.

UNIT 4: FOCUS ON WRITING

Dramas are intended to be performed, not read. When you write a drama, take into consideration the limitations of a live performance.

Writing a Dramatic Scene

A scene has the same form as a full-length play, with a beginning, a middle, and an end. Like a full-length play, it also includes stage directions and dialogue. Write a dramatic scene about a historical event or another topic of your choice.

The Writing Process

Good writing requires both time and effort. An effective writer completes a number of stages that together make up the writing process. The stages of the writing process are given below to help guide you through your assignment.

Prewriting

If you need help thinking of a topic, it is a good idea to brainstorm with classmates. List ideas that arise during the brainstorming session, and then decide on the one you would most like to write about.

After you have chosen a topic, consider whether your play will present a message or will be written just to entertain. What will be the setting of your play? List the characters and write a brief description of each one. If you look at *The Great American Justice Game*, you will notice that González-Pando provides character descriptions before Scene 1 opens.

Next, outline the plot, or sequence of events, that will take place in your scene. How will the scene begin? What is the central conflict, and how will you introduce it? What events follow as a result of this conflict? How does the scene end? Remember—you should include only events that can be presented on stage. Try to avoid situations that would be too difficult to create on stage.

Drafting and Revising

Begin by listing the characters, together with their descriptions. Following this list, write stage directions that include a detailed description of the setting.

As you write the first draft of your scene, refer to your lists and plot outline. Remember, this is just a first draft. You will have an opportunity to revise the scene in later drafts.

Write the scene in play format. The style used in *The Great American Justice Game* is standard: The character's name is at the left of the page, followed by a colon and the words the character says. Additional stage directions about actions or tone of voice are included in parentheses where needed. Try to keep each character's personality in mind as you write the dialogue. Would the character say the things you have written?

After you finish your first draft, you can begin the revision process. It is a good idea to read the dialogue aloud so that you can hear whether it sounds like natural conversation. Revise any sections you think sound unrealistic or have not made your meaning clear.

Proofreading and Publishing

During the proofreading stage, correct errors in spelling, grammar, punctuation, and capitalization. Then prepare a neat final copy.

Now your scene is ready for an audience! Choose actors from among your classmates and perform the scene for other classes in your school.

LITERATURE ACKNOWLEDGMENTS

ART ACKNOWLEDGMENTS

cover: New York City: Bird's-Eye View, Joaquin Torres-Garcia ca. 1920, *Yale University Art Gallery,* gift of Collection Societe Anonyme.

p. 3 Water Bearer, Victor Linares, *Museo del Barrio*

p. 49 Albonito, Pepe Cruz, *Museo del Barrio*

p. 101 Papiamento, Julio Larraz, *Nohra Haime Gallery*

p. 123 In Cayenas, Adolpho Piantini, courtesy of the artist